Card Games for One

Card Games for One

MICHAEL JOHNSTONE

WARD LOCK

795.4

Card games

A WARD LOCK BOOK

This edition published in the UK in 1994 by Ward Lock
Villiers House, 41/47 Strand, London WC2N 5JE

A Cassell Imprint

© Text and illustrations Ward Lock 1994

This book was previously published in 1989

Distributed in the United States
by Sterling Publishing Co., Inc.
387 Park Avenue South, New York, NY 10016-8810

Distributed in Australia
by Capricorn Link (Australia) Pty Ltd
2/13 Carrington Road, Castle Hill, NSW 2154

British Library Cataloguing-in-Publication Data
A catalogue record for this book is available from the British Library

ISBN 0-7063-7224-7

Typeset by Columns of Reading

Printed and bound in Great Britain

Cover photograph: Sue Atkinson.

CONTENTS

A LITTLE LIGHT ON THE SUBJECT

It is curious that although playing cards have long been used as an everyday pastime, experts are not sure where they originated. They think that it was in the east that people first amused themselves with cards. We know that they had reached England by 1496 for they are mentioned in the Parliamentary Rolls for that year.

Almost four hundred years later, in 1832, William IV granted royal letters patent for the manufacture of playing cards to Thomas de la Rue. It was he who first produced coloured high gloss playing cards.

At around the same time more and more people were forsaking candles as their main source of domestic lighting and installing gas lamps in their houses. Up until then people had tended to go to bed when darkness fell rather than use expensive candles by which to read, sew or write. Now with a cheap source of light, there was no need to retire at dusk and people found they had more leisure time, especially during the winter months. And so it is no coincidence that many of the card games with which we are familar were invented during the early years of Queen Victoria's reign.

Card games for one person were devised in Germany in the nineteenth century. They were probably introduced into England by officers returning from the Napoleonic Wars in Europe and many games that originate from this time have the Little Emperor's name in their title. It is interesting that, according to the Oxford English Dictionary, the word 'patience' was first used in a despatch from St Helena where Napoleon was in exile. His guards noted that Napoleon spent many hours 'playing patience'. But whether he was, in fact, playing true patience is doubtful, for it was a popular pastime in France to practise playing hands of whist on one's own, a game the French called *solitaire*.

At first, patience playing was restricted to a few fanatics in England, but when it was learned that Prince Albert himself was a keen and skilled player, the game increased in popularity and many new variations were invented. So the German prince who introduced the Christmas tree and other traditions we now associate with the typical English Christmas, was also responsible for popularizing something else from Germany that has been long regarded as typically English.

Around 1870 Lady Adelaide Cadogan compiled the first book of patience games. It was a slim volume, containing only 25 games, but it was an immediate and long lasting best-seller. Patience players look upon Lady Adelaide's book, *Illustrated Games of Patience*, as their bible, and Lady Adelaide herself their patron saint. As Lady Adelaide's husband was a member of parliament it is more than likely she acquired her skill as a patience player during the many nights she spent alone, waiting for him to return from late-night sittings at the House.

There are now over 500 games of patience and many variants. Some are so simple that they are literally child's play. Others demand skill, concentration and judgement. What they all have in common is the sense of achievement they give the player on these rare occasions when he beats the cards.

One English actress, a devoted patience player, referred to an invisible adversary when she wrote about patience, and that is part of the fun of the game. For no matter how often the invisible adversary triumphs, there is always the chance of one more shuffle and redeal. . . .

TECHNICAL TERMS

In describing the rules and method of play of games of patience, certain words crop up again and again. Here is a short alphabetical list of some words in the vocabulary of cards and their meaning.

Available cards are cards that can be played onto the tableau according to the rules of the game being played.

Building is playing cards in sequences according to the rules of the game. *Building up* is playing the cards in ascending order: *building down* is playing the cards in descending order. Building can be in suit, colour or alternate colour (e.g. if building down, the seven of hearts on the eight of clubs). In a few games, building can be up and down, and in some others, building is regardless of suit, e.g. any five on any six, if building down.

The cards are a standard 52-card pack in most games. In some games dealt with in a separate section of this book, two packs are used.

A column is a vertical line of cards each of which can either overlap the card above, or be in a space of its own.

A discard occurs when a card is laid aside for the duration of a game. In some games, certain cards are discarded before play begins. In such cases the pack is called a stripped pack.

Exposed cards are those cards at the end of a row or column or on top of a packet which are available.

A fan is made by counting cards off the top of the pack and spreading them in a fan shape on the table.

A file is a vertical column of built up cards in the layout. Cards within a file overlap each other in such a way that the suit and pip value of each card in the file can be seen. These columns are dealt from the point farthest from the player down towards the edge of the table nearest the player.

Foundation cards are those put to one side on which descending or ascending sequences are built, such sequences being called foundation piles or packets.

The layout or *tableau* is the way in which the cards are arranged according to the rules of the game.

A packet is a pile of cards.

Packing is placing suitable cards on the exposed ones in the layout.

Redeals are allowed in some games after the stock has been exhausted, cards in the talon (see below) becoming the stock.

Released cards are cards that become available for play during the course of a game, having previously been blocked by other cards on top of them.

A row is a line of cards parallel to the edge of the table where the player is seated, dealt from left to right with the cards overlapping each other in such a way that the suit and pip value of all the cards in the row are visible.

A sequence is the order in which the cards run. Sequences may run from, in ascending order, ace (low) up to king (high), or, in descending order, from king (high) to ace (low).

A space or *vacancy* is an unoccupied place in the layout in which a card may be legally played according to the rules of the game. In some games there are no fixed rules as to whether a space must be filled immediately or whether it may be left vacant until the player decides to fill it. Skilful play of vacancies is vital in getting some of the more complex games out.

The stock is the part of the pack remaining after the tableau has been laid out. These are the cards used to play the game.

Tableau see Layout.

The talon is formed by cards turned up in the course of play which are not available for play according to the rules of the game. It is often called the waste pile. In some games once the stock is exhausted, the talon is dealt again.

Two more things before before we start describing the rules and method of play for the 100 patience games contained in this book. Firstly, in the course of playing many of them (and in some cases in laying out the tableau) quite a lot of space is required. And although it is possible to play all the games with standard packs of cards, it is better to invest in packs of patience cards. These are smaller than standard-sized cards, so the games can be played on a smaller surface area than would otherwise be needed: and they are also easier to handle.

Secondly, where the word difficult is mentioned in describing a game, this does not indicate that the game is hard to master (although it may well be!) but that it does not come out as often as many others. Don't be put off by this. The sense of achievement when the old adversary is beaten and a 'difficult' game comes out is immensely satisfying.

SIMPLE ONE-PACK GAMES

ACCORDION

Deal all the cards face up in one long row. If the game comes out, the player is left with all the cards in one pile. A card can be moved onto the card on its left if it matches it in suit or pip value: so the nine of clubs, say, could be moved to the left if the card next to it is a club or a nine. When playing the third card from the left, it is within the rules to skip the card on its left and put on the far left hand card if it matches.

As piles are created, the top card designates the suit and pip value of the pile which can be moved according to the rules of the game.

ALTERNATE

Remove the two red aces and two black kings from the pack and lay them on the table, ace of hearts on the left, then the king of clubs followed by the ace of diamonds with the king of spades on the right. These are the foundation cards on which piles are built in alternate colours in ascending order on the aces and in descending order on the kings.

Deal the cards one at a time, building where possible, or discarding into any of four waste heaps. The top card of each waste pile is always available. When all the cards have been dealt, take the piles into hand and without shuffling them, redeal. Two such redeals are allowed.

AULD LANG SYNE

Remove the four aces from a pack of cards and lay them in a row. These are the foundation cards on which suits are built up in sequence.

Deal a line of four cards below the four aces, playing any twos that are dealt onto their aces. Descending sequences of alternate colour are created in this layout. So, for example, if a red seven and a black eight are dealt in the first row, the seven can be placed on the eight, before dealing a second line of four cards below the first, with the cards overlapping. Vacancies that are created remain until the are filled during the next deal. The game continues in this manner until all the cards have been dealt, always in rows of four. Only the bottom cards in each file can be moved, either on to the foundation piles or on to other files as described above.

BARONESS

Deal a row of five cards and discard any pair that total thirteen with jacks counting eleven, queens twelve and aces one. Kings are discarded on their own. Now deal another five cards on top of the first five, again discarding single kings and pairs totalling thirteen. The top card of each pile is available. The last two cards are dealt to the side the tableau and are still available.

BLOCK ELEVEN

Deal a tableau of twelve cards in three rows of four cards each. Any court cards, apart from aces (which count as one), that are in the final tableau should be removed and put to the bottom of the pack. Spaces created are filled from the pack. If any further court cards turn up in filling the gaps created, these are also put to the bottom of the pack and replaced and so on until the tableau contains nothing but non-court cards. If the original tableau contains no court cards, the first one turned up in the course of play must be put to the bottom of the pack. Cover each pair of cards that total eleven in the tableau with cards from the stock. When a court card is dealt to the tableau, it blocks play on the pile to which it is played.

The game is won when the stock is exhausted and each pile in the tableau is topped with a court card.

CANFIELD

Canfield is probably the only patience that started off as a gambling game. It is named after the owner of a casino in Saratoga in the United States where players could buy a pack of cards for $50 and use it to play a hand of the game under the close scrutiny of the croupier who paid $5 for every card in the foundation piles at the end of the game or $500 if the player got the game out. The game came to be called after Canfield who made a fortune out of it.

Shuffle the pack, count off the top thirteen cards and place them face up on your left as the stock. The fourteenth card is the first foundation and should be placed above and to the right of the stock. Then start the tableau, dealing a line of four cards to the right of the stock, the first card under the first foundation card. The other three foundation cards are the cards of the same rank as the first one and should be placed next to the first foundation card as they are turned up. Foundation piles are built upwards in suit sequence. So, for example, if the foundations were nines, the sequence would be nine, ten, jack, queen, king, ace, two and so on up to eight.

Descending sequences of alternate colour are packed on the tableau. Only the bottom card on a file is available for play either on its foundation or onto a suitable card in the tableau. Suitable sequences in the tableau can by played onto an appropriate exposed card: e.g. if there was a

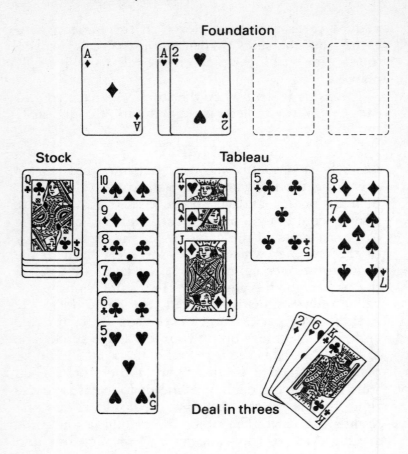

descending sequence of black ten down to red three, the whole pile could be played onto a red jack. This is useful in creating vacancies in the tableau.

The 34 cards that remain after the stock, first foundation and four tableau cards have been dealt, should be placed face down in front of the player who turns over the first three cards and lays them face up alongside the hand. Only the top card is available and can be played either onto a foundation pile or to the tableau according to the rules of the game. If it is playable, the next card becomes playable in turn. Once all possible cards have been played, the next three cards from the hand are turned over and placed face up on top of what is now the talon.

When the hand is exhausted, the talon is turned over without being shuffled and becomes the new hand, the cards in it again being turned over in packets of three. There is no limit to the number of times this can be done.

A space in the tableau must be filled by the top card in the stock or, if the stock is exhausted, by the top card in the talon.

The rules of the game have changed since the days when anxious gamblers pitted their wits against the cards in Mr Canfield's gambling den. Then, they turned the cards in hand over one at a time with no redeal. But the house won so often that before long there were few takers: so Canfield gave players the choice of either playing to the original rules or turning over the cards three at a time with two redeals allowed. Even then he continued to make a fortune.

CASTLES IN SPAIN

Shuffle and cut a pack of cards. Deal a row of five cards, face down from left to right; then a row of four cards above the first; a row of three cards above that and finally one card above the centre card of the third row. Now deal two more complete sets of cards face down on top of the cards on the table, following the same pattern as before. The last thirteen cards are dealt face up on top of the existing piles, again following the same pattern. The piles are the depots. Any aces showing are played to the foundation row once the tableau is complete; the card beneath the ace is turned up and becomes available.

The aim of Castles in Spain is to build up on the foundation cards strictly in suit. Available cards may be played either on their appropriate foundation pile or in descending sequence of alternate colour on another depot. Sequences or part sequences can be moved from one depot to another or to fill any spaces that are created. Such spaces must be filled. There is no redeal.

DOUBLET

Deal the cards into twelve packets of three cards each, face downwards. On top of each packet deal another card, face up. The remaining four cards are put to one side, face down, to make the reserve. If any of the exposed cards are of the same pip or court value, discard them and turn up the cards underneath. And so the game proceeds, looking for and discarding pairs. When a whole packet has been exhausted, the vacancy is filled by the top card in the reserve. The aim, of course, is to end up with no cards in the tableau and with an exhausted reserve.

GOLF

Deal seven columns of five overlapping cards and place one extra card beneath this tableau to start the talon. The aim of Golf is to play all the cards from the tableau on to the talon either in descending or ascending sequence regardless of suit. Thus if a four was the card in the talon, an available five from the tableau could be played on it, followed by a six, then another five and another six, and so on. The only exceptions are that only a two can be built on an ace and a king stops a sequence (i.e. a king can be played on a queen, but not a queen on a king). When there are no more plays to be made, turn over the next card from the stock, lay it face up on the talon and start again.

KLONDIKE

Deal a row of seven cards, face down. Now, starting on the second card from the left, deal a second, overlapping row, this time of six cards. This is followed by a row of five cards, starting on the third card from the left and so on until there are seven files of one, two, three, four, five, six and seven cards. Turn over the last card in each file.

The foundation cards are the aces on which complete suits are to be built up in ascending order. Any aces showing at this stage should be taken from the file and placed in a row beyond the tableau.

Sequences of cards of alternate colours in descending order are built up within the tableau – red eight on black nine, black nine on a red ten and so on. Whenever a card or a sequence of cards is moved from one file to another, the face down card beneath is turned over and is now available for play.

Once a card has been played onto its foundation pile, it may not be returned to the tableau. Spaces created within the tableau can only be filled by a king or a sequence with a king as the base card. (Some players bend this rule.)

Once all possible moves in the tableau have been made, turn over the cards in the stock one by one, playing any cards that can be played onto a suitable card in the tableau or onto its foundation pile. Cards that cannot be played are put in the talon.

One redeal is allowed (but here, again, some players allow themselves two, three, four, or an infinite number of redeals). Some players also vary the rules in the way they play the stock, turning over three cards at a time. In such cases, only the top card is immediately available. Only if it can be played does the one beneath it become available. And if the second card can be played, the third card is available.

There are several variations of Klondike.

Joker Klondike is played with a joker added to the pack. Whenever it becomes available it has to be played onto a foundation pile, assuming the suit and value of the next card in that sequence. Available cards can be played on top of the joker. When the card for which it stands becomes available, it is put in its proper place and the joker put on top of another foundation file, again assuming the suit and value of the next card is in sequence. If no foundation has been begun by the time the joker is turned up, it cannot be moved from its position until an ace appears and is played to the foundation row.

Multiple Klondike is played by two or more players each playing their own simultaneous games of Klondike with packs of different design, but playing to common foundation piles.

If players try to play to the same foundation pile at the same time, the player whose card is in position wins: the others must return their card to the tableau (or to their talon).

MARRIAGE

Remove a king and a queen from the pack and shuffle the rest of the cards. Put the king on the bottom of the pack and the queen on the top. The cards are now dealt in a row. Whenever a card is flanked by cards of the same suit or pip value, it is discarded and the card on its right moved to the left to fill the space created. The aim of the game is to discard all the cards except the queen (the first card to be dealt) and the king (the last one) so joining them together in happy marriage.

A variation of the game allows one and two cards flanked by cards of the same suit and value to be discarded.

MONTE CARLO

Suits play no part in this patience that depends entirely on the cards' pip values. The layout is made up of twenty cards in five columns of four cards each. If two cards of the same value are alongside each other either vertically, diagonally or horizontally they are removed from the layout. Spaces in upper rows are filled by moving up the cards below them. Cards are then dealt from the pack to bring the number of cards in the layout back to twenty and play continues in the same way until all the cards in the pack have been paired off.

Only two cards can be removed. If three cards of matching value adjoin, it is up to the player to decide which pair he wants to remove.

OLD PATIENCE

The aim of Old Patience is to find the four aces and, using them as foundation cards, build up four sequences ace to king regardless of suit value.

Deal the top card from the pack to the table and turn it face up. If its an ace, put it in the foundation row. If not turn over the next card, and the next and so on, creating four files on the table. Cards that cannot be played to the foundation row can be played to any of the files on the table. Cards cannot be played to the foundations from the table until all the cards in the pack have been turned over and either played to an appropriate foundation pile or put in any of the four files.

PADDY'S DELIGHT

This is also known as Shamrocks. Deal the whole pack into seventeen fans of three cards, each spread out so that all cards within each fan are visible. If in the course of laying out the tableau, a king is found to be above another card of the same suit within a fan, put it below that card. The last card forms a 'fan' on its own. The uncovered card of each fan is available for play and can be played onto another available card either in upward or downward sequence regardless of suit. But no fan is ever allowed to contain more than three cards, so the first move *must* be onto the one card fan. When aces become available, they are put in a foundation row above the tableau. Foundations ascend in suit sequence from ace to king.

If an entire fan is exhausted, the space created remains empty.

POKER PATIENCE

Turn over the top 25 cards from the pack and make them into five poker hands. Lay the best hand in a row, with the second best below it, the third below it, the fourth below that, with the worst hand making up the bottom row. Score the hands as follows.

A Royal Flush (Ace, King, Queen, Jack and ten of a suit) .... 35 points
A Straight Flush (five consecutive cards of the same suit) .... 30 points
Four of a kind (four aces or whatever) 15 points
Full House (three of a kind and a pair).. 10 points
Flush (five cards of the same suit).......... 7 points
Straight run (five consecutive cards of different suits)... 6 points
Three of a kind.................................... 5 points
Two pairs .... 2 points
One pair .... 1 point
Face cards high (no pairs)...................... 0 points

Players set their own target score. A score of 80 or over is excellent.

SHIP SHAPE AND BRISTOL FASHION

Deal the tableau, eight fans of three cards each, arranged in two rows of four fans each, with a reasonable space between each fan. Below the tableau deal a row of three cards – the reserve. All cards are face up.

Aces are removed to a foundation row above the tableau when they become available. Building in foundation is upwards regardless of suit. Packing within the tableau is downwards, regardless of suit, the right hand card of each fan being available. Only one card at a time can be played from a fan either for packing or building. Spaces in the tableau caused by the removal of an entire fan remain vacant.

The stock is dealt three cards at a time, one card on top of each reserve pile. The top cards on each reserve pile are available for building on the foundations or packing within the tableau. There is no redeal.

SON OF FORTUNE

Put the four aces in a foundation row. Sequences are built up in suits on the appropriate foundation pile. The tableau is made up of two rows of six cards each. No moves can be made until the tableau has been laid out, but once it is complete, any cards that can be played according to the rules of the game are played. The vacancies thus created are filled by the top card from the stock. Suit sequences are built down within the tableau. Only one card at a time can be played from the top of a pile in the tableau either on to a foundation or on to another pile in the tableau. Turn the cards in the stock over one at a time. Suitable cards are played to the tableau or the foundation piles. Cards that cannot be played are put in the waste pile, the top card of which is available for play. A space created in the tableau is filled by a card from the waste pile or from the stock if the waste pile is exhausted. There is no redeal, but nonetheless Son of Fortune comes out surprisingly often, which makes a refreshing change for there are some games of patience that rarely allow the player a victory.

TRAVELLING MEN

Deal a row of four cards face down and not over-lapping. Beneath it deal a second row, also of four cards, followed by a third so that you have twelve cards, face down on the table. Deal a second card on each pile, then a third and finally a fourth so that you create twelve piles of four cards each and have four cards left in hand. Place these face down beneath the third row, a little left of centre. These are the eponymous travelling men.

The only difficulty in this game is that you have to imagine that each pile is numbered. The top row, 1 – 4, left to right. The middle row 5 – 8, left to right and the bottom row 9 – 12, again left to right.

Play begins by turning over the top card and placing it face up under its appropriate pile – an ace under pile 1, a five under pile 5 and so on – turn over the top card of that pile and put it face up under its appropriate pile. For the purposes of the game, jacks are counted as 11 and queens as 12. There is no pile under which to put a king, so any kings that are turned up are placed face up to the right of the travelling men, and the top traveller is revealed and played. The game comes to an end if the four kings are turned up before all the other face-down cards have been revealed and played, because, when the fourth king is played to its pile, the travelling men are exhausted and there is no card in their pile to continue the game.

This game can also be played by dealing a circle of

twelve cards and putting the thirteenth card in the middle before continuing to put cards in the circle until you have a circle of four-card piles representing 1 – 12 on a clock face and the four pile travelling men in the middle. Jacks are played to eleven o'clock and queens to twelve o'clock. Kings are played to the centre pile.

TRIPLETS

Deal the cards, face down, into sixteen packets of three cards each and two packets of two cards each. Turn over the top card of each packet and search for three cards of consecutive value, regardless of suit. Remove them and expose the cards underneath. Continue in the same way. If the game comes out you will have seventeen sets of triplets. Kings can be married with jacks and queens to make runs of jack, queen, king, or with aces and twos to make runs of king, ace, two.

It helps to get the game out if, when you have two cards of the same rank available for play, you choose the one from the packet containing more cards than the other.

TUTENKHAMEN'S TOMB

Remove a king from the pack and lay it on the table to represent Tutenkhamen's Tomb at the peak of a pyramid. Complete the tableau by dealing twenty-seven cards face up as follows: two cards in a row beneath Tutenkhamen's Tomb, followed by rows of three, four, five, six cards, with a base row of seven cards. Keep a space between cards within the same row, but overlap each row with the one above so that each card is partially covered by two cards in the row below.

At the outset of the game, only the cards on the base row are available and are removed in pairs that total thirteen: kings are removed singly as they count thirteen; queens count twelve and jacks eleven. So, if in the bottom row at the start of the game, there's a jack and a two, or any other pair that total thirteen, they are removed, forming the start of the discard pile.

Cards in the upper rows of the pyramid become available when the two adjacent cards in the row beneath them are played. Available cards in the tableau can be paired with one another if their total pip value is thirteen and discarded

The stock is turned over one card at a time. If the card from the stock can be married with an available card to total thirteen, both cards are put into the discard pile. Cards that cannot be paired are played to a separate waste pile, the top card of which is available for pairing.

The game is won when (and if) the waste pile contains all the cards in the pack apart from Tutenkhamen's Tomb which lies on the table in solitary splendour. There is no redeal.

DIFFICULT ONE-PACK GAMES

AGNES

Deal out twenty-eight cards in seven rows face upwards – seven cards in the top row, six in the second and so on, until the left-hand column contains seven cards and the right-hand column is made up of one card. Turn over the next, twenty-ninth card, and put it in a foundation row above the tableau.

The other foundation cards are the cards of the same rank as the first and are played to the foundation row when they become available. Foundations are built up in ascending suit sequence. Pack descending colour sequences on the exposed card of each column. These packed sequences can only be moved *en bloc* onto an exposed card if they are all of the same suit. Only the exposed cards can be built onto the foundations.

After all building and packing has been done, deal seven cards, one to the bottom of each column, filling any vacant columns that have been created during initial play with the card beneath the empty column. Once all possible builds and packing have been made, deal another seven cards in the same way but before you do so this time it is permissible to fill vacant columns with any exposed card. Again make all possible builds and packings before dealing a final row of seven cards. Should any cards remaining from the first deal become exposed, then they immediately become available once more. When all possible moves have been made, turn over the last two cards and play them to the tableau before continuing to pack and build on the foundation piles.

THE BATTLE OF THE LADIES

Remove the four queens and four jacks from the pack. Discard three of the jacks and lay the remaining one at the top of the table. Put the four queens in a row at the bottom of the table: then take the top six cards from the pack and lay them face up on the table to form a pyramid with the four queens forming the base, the six cards forming the two sides (three on each side), with the jack as the apex. Cards in the pyramid are packed downwards in

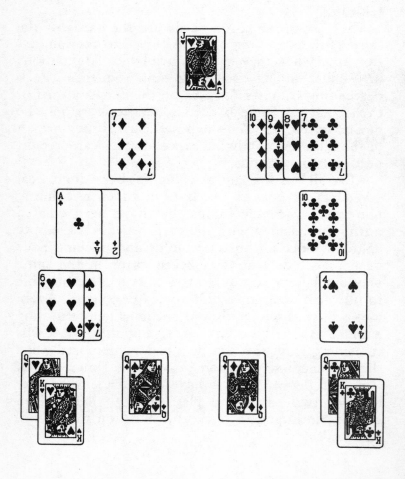

alternate colours and on the queens they are built upwards in suit sequence. The jack remains uncovered throughout the game, the queen whose foundation is completed first, claims the jack and wins.

Cards on the sides of the pyramid are all available either for packing on each other or for building. Cards may only be moved singly. Spaces created are filled by cards from the stock. When no more moves are possible, deal another six cards to the the sides of the pyramid, completing the deal before making any further builds or packs. Continue in the same way until the stock is exhausted. If, by this time, no queen has claimed the jack, take the packets forming the sides of the wall into hand, putting the packet at the bottom of the left wall on top of the packet at the bottom of the right wall, then putting them on top of the next packet of the left wall and so on. The new stock is not shuffled.

There are two redeals.

THE BELEAGUERED CASTLE

Remove the four aces from the pack and lay them face up in a foundation column. Foundation piles are built up in suits. Now deal a card to the left and right of each ace and not overlapping them. Continue to deal to the left and right of each ace, so that you have four rows of thirteen cards, laid out as in the diagram. Only the outermost cards in each row are available for play. They can be played to their foundation pile if possible. Cards within the rows become available when the cards blocking them are moved in creating descending sequences of alternate colours. Cards can only be moved singly, never in sequences. In the diagram on page 28 the two of spades can be played to its foundation pile, then the three of spades onto the two. The queen of diamonds can now be played onto the king of clubs, the ten of diamonds onto the jack of spades, seven of spades onto the eight of diamonds and so on.

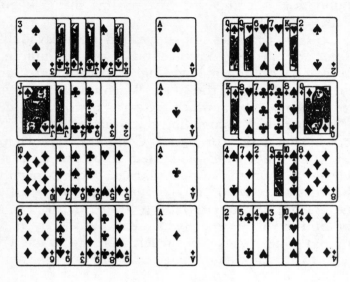

BISLEY

Lay the four aces in a row and then deal nine cards to the right of them, creating a row of thirteen cards in all. Deal the rest of the pack into columns of three cards each beneath the top row. The completed tableau will have four rows of thirteen cards each in vertical columns of four cards each. Foundation piles are built upwards in suit with the aces as the foundation cards.

The bottom cards of each column are available for play, they can be played onto their appropriate foundation if possible or they can be played onto the bottom card of another column if it matches it in suit and is next to it in rank. So, the eight of clubs can be played on either the nine or the seven of clubs. If it has been played on the nine, it can later be moved and played on the seven if need be.

Any kings that become available are removed and placed above their matching aces. Suit sequences are built down on them. When a column becomes empty it is not filled.

It takes some skill to avoid blocking builds by trapping vital cards within a column. Skilled Bisley players can tell after studying the layout for a few seconds if there are any automatic blocks that will prevent the game coming out. If this is the case, leave the four aces where they are, take the rest of the cards into hand, shuffle them and redeal the layout.

CALCULATION

Aces count as one, jacks as eleven, queens as twelve, kings as thirteen and other cards as their pip value in this simple but fascinating game.

Place any ace, any two, any three and any four on the table. These are the foundation cards on which piles are created as follows:

1.	1,2,3,4,5,6,7,8,9,10,11,12,13.
2.	2,4,6,8,10,12,1,3,5,7,9,11,13.
3.	3,6,9,12,2,5,8,11,1,4,7,10,13.
4.	4,8,12,3,7,11,2,6,10,1,5,9,13.

Once the foundation cards have been laid down, shuffle the rest of the pack and turn the cards over one by one, playing to foundation piles if possible.

Cards that cannot be played are put face up in discard piles below the foundations. There are four such piles and discards can be played to any of them. But once a card is in a discard pile, it cannot be transferred to another one. The top card in each discard pile is available. Thankfully, it is permissible to spread the discard piles out to refresh the memory as to which cards they contain, but only the top card is available.

CHESSBOARD

This game follows the rules of play for Fortress (see page 32) but the player has the choice of foundation cards which are placed in the space between the two flanks. After the tableau has been dealt, look at it carefully before electing the rank of the foundations, choosing a rank that will promote plenty of play within the tableau. If it is decided that sixes are to be the foundations, the suit sequence would run 6, 7, 8, 9, 10, J, Q, K, A, 2, 3, 4 and 5.

CROSSWORD

Remove the twelve court cards from the pack, shuffle the remainder (now the stock) and put the top card face up anywhere on the table. Other cards are turned over one by one and played so that they sit either above, below, on either side of or at one of the four corners of a card already played. Once a card has been played it cannot be moved.

The aim of Crossword is to end up with a square of seven cards each way, the pip value of each column and file adding up to an even number. The court cards which count zero are played whenever the player wishes to play them, serving as stops just as the black squares in a crossword indicate where a word starts and finishes. The pip value of the cards within stops must also add up to an even number.

If the game progresses well, when 48 cards have been played, there will be one vacant space within the crossword grid. If all the stops have been used, there will be four cards in the stock, or there will be three cards in the stock and one stop, two cards in the stock and two stops, one card in the stock and three stops, or no cards in the stock and four stops. Any cards remaining in the stock are turned face up and the player chooses which of the four cards left to play to complete the game.

CZARINA

Players often become so frustrated in playing Czarina that they begin to wonder if it can ever come out. The knowledge that it must occasionally do so, tempts them to try just one more game, then another. . .

Shuffle the cards then turn over the top card – the first foundation card – and play it to the top left of the table. The other three foundations are the three other cards of the same value and are played to the table when they become available during play. The second foundation is placed alongside the first but some distance from it: the third is placed beneath the first again some distance from it: the fourth completes the square.

As soon as the first foundation card is in position, proceed to deal the tableau – five cards in a cross formation - a row of three cards, the central one of which is the central card of a three card column.

Building on foundation cards is upwards in suit sequence: packing on the tableau is downwards regardless of suit. The stock is turned over one card at a time, suitable cards being used for building or packing, unplayable cards being played to the waste pile. Cards within the tableau can be packed on each other and when a vacancy occurs it is filled by the next card from the pack or the top card in the talon which is always available.

If, when all the cards have been played, the foundation piles are complete it is a rare victory. But if this has not been achieved, one privilege remains. The talon is gathered up and the top two cards turned over: if either can be played the game can continue, the unplayable card being the first card in the talon for the redeal. If neither card can be played, there is nothing for it but to take all the cards into hand, shuffle them and start again.

FORTRESS

Chessboard (see page 30) is similar to this game. Deal the cards so that you have two rows of six overlapping cards and four rows of five cards below them. Leave at least a card space between the two flanks. The right hand card of each row is available and can be played onto the right hand card of another row according to the rules of the game.

Cards are played within the tableau in suit sequence, either up or down. Aces, when they become available, are placed in the space between the two flanks as foundation cards on which suit sequences are built up.

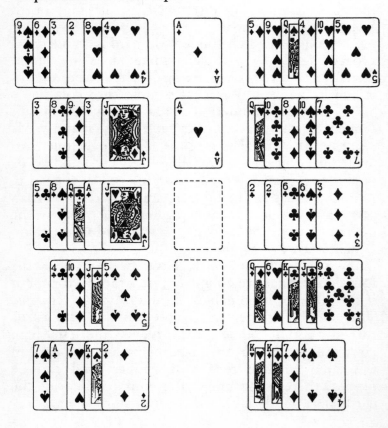

FOUR SEASONS

Deal five cards into a cross shape, placing three cards in a row and adding one card each above and below the centre card. The first foundation is the sixth card which is dealt to one of the corners of the cross. Put the other three foundation cards (those of the same rank) in the other corners when they become available. The foundations are built up in suits, the aces being played after the kings.

Turn over cards from the stock one by one. Cards that cannot be played are discarded. The top card of the waste pile is always available. Cards in the tableau are built down regardless of suit, kings being played on aces where aces are not foundation cards. Spaces in the tableau can be filled by any available card. There is no redeal.

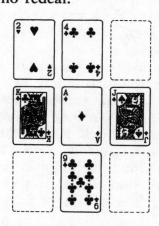

GRANDPA'S CLOCK

Remove the two of hearts, three of spades, four of diamonds, five of clubs, six of hearts, seven of spades, eight of diamonds, nine of clubs, ten of hearts, jack of spades, queen of diamonds and the king of clubs from the pack and lay them in a circle one card at each hour on a clock face. The two of hearts goes at five o'clock, the three at six and so on with the king at four o'clock. These are the foundation cards on which suits are built up in sequence until the sequence reaches the number of the hours at which the foundation cards sit.

The rest of the pack is dealt face down into five rows of eight cards each, with the cards of each row overlapping slightly. The bottom card of each file is available for play on the foundation or within the tableau, building downwards regardless of suit.

Spaces made when the last card in a file is played can be filled by any available card.

IT FOLLOWS

The rule of this game is that cards may only be placed on each other in the order hearts, clubs, diamonds, spades. So only a heart can be played on a club and so on. The game cannot come out if the sequence is broken.

Lay out a row of six cards. If any of the cards can be packed in a downward sequence according to the rule of the game, do so, filling vacant spaces from the pack. Any aces that turn up should be played to the foundation row which goes from left to right in the order ace of hearts, clubs, diamonds, spades.

The rule of suit sequence applies to the ascending sequences on the foundation piles, too. So the ace of diamond foundation would run ace of diamonds, two of spades, three of hearts, four of clubs, five of diamonds. . .

Cards from the stock are turned over one at a time and can be played either onto the tableau or the foundation if suitable. Otherwise they are put in the waste pile, the top card of which is available. There is no redeal.

If the game comes out, the completed foundation piles will be topped from left to right with the kings of hearts, clubs, diamonds and spades.

LITTLE SPIDER

Remove the two red aces and two black kings from the pack and put them on the table as the foundation cards. Foundation piles are built in ascending suit sequence on the aces and in descending suit sequence on the kings.

The first eight cards from the stock are now dealt in two rows of four cards each, one above the foundations and one below. During the deal, any suitable card in the top row can be played onto its foundation pile, but cards dealt to the lower row can only be played to their foundations if they are dealt directly below them. After all the cards have been dealt this restriction is withdrawn and any suitable card can be played to its foundation.

After each eight card deal, the top card on each pile is available and can be played to foundation piles (according to the rules described above) or packed onto one of the other piles. Packing can be in either descending or ascending order but once the direction for a particular pile has been decided it cannot be changed. Packing is continuous, aces below twos and above kings: i.e. in a descending sequence the order would be 3,2,A,K,Q . . . and in an ascending sequence it would be Q,K,A,2,3 . . . Vacancies created in the course of play are not filled.

MAZE

Deal the pack into two eight-card and four nine-card rows and then remove the four kings from the tableau and discard them. This leaves four spaces within the tableau. The aim of Maze is to use these four spaces and the two spaces at the right end of the two eight-card rows to move cards within the tableau, one card at a time, so that if the game comes out the maze is constructed of four ascending suit sequences starting with an ace as the extreme left-hand card in the top row and finishing with a queen at the right-end of the bottom row. Sequences follow from the right-hand end of one row to the left-hand end of the row beneath: i.e. if the card at the end of one row is the eight of hearts, the card at the other end of the row beneath should be the nine of hearts. During play, the top row is a continuation of the bottom one.

Cards can be moved into vacant spaces only if they are either one higher of the same suit as the card on the left, or one lower of the same suit as the card on the right.

The only exception to the rules occurs when a space is created on the right of a queen: it may be filled by any ace although it is not obligatory to do so, as it may be better to move the card that is one lower of the same suit as the card on the right of the space.

OSMOSIS

Deal four piles of four cards each, face down, in a column. Neaten them and turn them over so that only the top card of each pile can be seen. These are the reserve piles. Deal the next card, the first foundation card, to the right of the top reserve pile. The other foundations are the cards of the same rank as the first and are played as they become available to the right of the other reserve piles in descending order. Foundations are built in suit, regardless of sequence. Cards played to the foundations should overlap the one immediately beneath so that all cards in the foundation piles are visible. It is essential that the player can see all the cards in the foundations because a card cannot be played to its foundation unless a card of the same rank has been played to the foundation above. For example, if the top foundation card is the eight of hearts, the second the eight of spades and the queen and five of hearts have been played to heart foundation, only the queen and five of spades can be played on the spade foundation.

The top cards in the reserve piles are always available for play according to the rules. The stock is turned over in batches of three, the top card of which is available. The order of the cards must not be disturbed in counting off the batches. If the top card of a batch can be played, the one under it becomes available and so on. Unplayable cards from the hand are put in the waste pile which becomes the stock when the original stock is exhausted.

As many redeals are allowed as are necessary until all the cards in the stock and reserves have been played to their foundations or the game becomes obviously blocked.

A version of the games called **Open Osmosis** allows the cards in the reserve piles to be played in such a way that all the cards therein are visible. This version comes out much more often than the parent game as knowledge of all the cards in the reserve gives players the chance to avoid the blocks inevitable in Osmosis.

PERPETUAL MOTION

Deal the cards into thirteen packets of four cards each, face up, laying out the packets as a row of six packets above a lower row of seven packets. Mentally number the packets one to thirteen, packet one being the left hand packet in the top row, packet seven the left hand column in the lower row with the seventh packet in the lower row being packet thirteen. For the purposes of the game, jacks count as eleven, queens as twelve and kings as thirteen.

Begin by moving the top card on packet one to the bottom of packet two, then the top card of packet two to the bottom of packet three and so on, the top card of packet thirteen going under packet one.

When a packet is topped by a card of its own number, it takes no further part in the round. In order to be able to continue, place the top card on the packet on its left under the packet on its right.

If, at the beginning of the game, an ace tops pile number one, start by taking the top card from pile 13 and placing it under pile 2. The first round continues until each packet is topped by a card of its own number at which point these top cards are removed and discarded. The last card removed from the top of its packet is still in hand. Begin the second round by playing it under the packet of its own number, and putting the top card from that packet under the next.

A win is achieved by discarding three sets of thirteen cards, leaving thirteen cards in the tableau.

PRINCE ALBERT

Deal a row of nine cards face up, followed by a row of eight cards starting on the second card on the left, the cards in the second row overlapping the cards in the first row. Continue with a row of seven cards starting with the third card on the left and so on until there are nine columns in the layout, one card in the left hand column and nine cards in the right hand column. The other seven cards are placed face up in a reserve between the player and the layout so that all are available. The available cards are those at the bottom of each column and all the cards in the reserve. Available cards can only be played one at a time on a card of a different colour and one above it in value. Sequences cannot be moved. When aces become available, they are moved to the foundation row above the tableau. Foundation piles are built up in suits.

Cards from the reserve may be played either onto the appropriate foundation or onto the layout according to the rules, but once a card has been played from the reserve, it may not be returned to it. Empty columns can be filled with any available card.

QUADRILLE

Cards are turned up from the stock one at a time. The foundation cards, which are played to the tableau as they turn up are the four fives and the four sixes arranged in a circle with the fives at North, South, East and West, and the sixes sitting at an angle between them. Suit sequences are built on them as follows:

On the fives build down to aces followed by the kings: on the sixes build up to jacks.

Queens play no part in the game. When they turn up they are played to the middle of the tableau.

Two redeals are allowed after the stock is exhausted.

RAGLAN

Remove the four aces from the pack and put them in a foundation row, beneath which the tableau is dealt, face down into nine columns, the cards within each column overlapping slightly. There are nine cards in the top row, eight in the second row, and so on until the seventh row where only three cards are dealt. There are are then seven cards in the first three columns, six cards in the fourth column, five in the fifth, four in the sixth, three in the seventh, two in the eighth and the extreme right hand column is a single card. Turn over the bottom card of each column. These cards are available for play. The remaining stock of six cards should now be dealt, face up, in a row beneath the tableau. These cards are also available for play but only to the foundation piles (on which cards are built in ascending suit sequences), not to the tableau. Available cards in the tableau can be packed in descending sequences of alternate colour. Cards can only be moved singly: sequences and part-sequences cannot be moved. As columns become empty during the course of play they may be filled with any available card.

SCORPION

Deal a row of seven cards, the first four face downwards, the next three face up. Deal three more rows in the same way, and then four rows of seven cards, all face up. Each card should slightly overlap the one above it. Put the remaining three cards face down to one side for the moment.

The foundation cards are the four kings, which stay within the tableau, and on which descending suit sequences are built. Cards within the tableau may be packed on top of the bottom card of each column if the bottom card is the one above them in the same suit. But when a card is moved, all the cards below it in its column must also be moved. So, if the eight of hearts is the bottom card of a column and the seven of hearts is covered by two other cards, all three cards are moved onto the eight.

When a face-down card becomes the bottom card in a column, it is turned over and can now be packed or packed on. Empty columns must be filled by a king and all the cards below it in its column. When all possible moves have been made, the remaining three cards are dealt face up to the bottom of the three leftmost columns and the game continues until it is totally blocked.

STOREHOUSE

Remove the four twos from the pack and put them in the foundation row. Suit sequences are built up to aces on the foundation cards. Deal thirteen cards to a pile below the foundation row and to the left of it. These cards are the storehouse which gives the game its name. Deal a row of four cards to the right of the storehouse to form the tableau.

Cards in the stock are turned over one card at a time. They are played to the foundation if possible, or to the tableau, which is packed in descending suit sequence. Keep the bottom card showing as an entire pile can be put on top of another pile if possible during the course of play. Cards that cannot be played are put face up in a waste pile. Spaces that are created must be filled immediately with the top card from the storehouse, unless it is exhausted. If that happens spaces are filled by the top card of the waste pile or the next card from the stock according to the player's wishes.

The top cards in the tableau, storehouse and waste pile are all available for play.

Two redeals are allowed.

THE TOWER OF PISA

This patience game makes use of nine cards only and if it works out (and after some thought it usually does despite the seemingly insolvable problems that crop up) the player is left with a single file of cards descending in sequence from ten to two.

To start, remove a ten, nine, eight, seven, six, five, four, three and two from a pack of cards, shuffle them and lay them out in three columns of three cards each. (The diagram is merely an example and the sequence of cards should not be followed.)The rest of the pack is discarded. The aim of the game is, as already said, to form the cards into a single file in correct descending order. Only the bottom card of a column can be moved and it can only be placed at the bottom of another column under a card of higher value. An empty file can be filled by the bottom card of either of the other two files.

The first problem in the hand below is to get the ten into the top row. This can be done by putting the four under the ten, the seven under the eight, the four under the seven, the two under the four. The ten can now be moved to fill the empty centre file. Now the cards have to be manipulated so that the nine is under the ten, the eight under the nine and so on, always playing according to the rules.

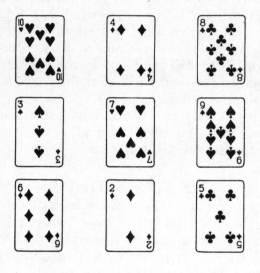

TWO-PACK GAMES

ALTERNATIONS

Shuffle the packs together and deal a row of seven cards, face up. Beneath this and overlapping the cards in the top row slightly, deal a second row, face down, then another row face up and so on until there are seven columns of seven cards each, the first, third, fifth and seventh cards in which are all face up.

The foundation cards are the eight aces which are played to the foundation row above the tableau as they become available in play. Foundations are built up in suit sequence. Packing in the tableau is downwards, regardless of suit. Complete and part sequences can be packed onto suitable cards in the tableau. When the cards blocking a face-down card are removed, it is turned over and becomes available.

When all possible packing and building has been done with the cards in the tableau, the stock is turned over one card at a time, unusable cards being played to the waste pile.

Vacant columns can be filled with any available card in the tableau, a complete or part sequence, the next card of the stock or the top card in the talon. There is no redeal.

ANGEL'S HARP

Deal out a row of eight cards, face down, with a ninth card face up at the end of it. Beneath the top row and placed so that they don't overlap, deal a row of seven face-down cards, with an eighth face up at the end, and so on down to a bottom row that consists of one, face-up, card. Any exposed ace should be removed to the foundation row where the cards ascend in suit sequence to king. The other aces are played to the foundation zone when they become available.

When the exposed card at the end of a row is played, the card beside it is turned over and becomes available either for building on the foundations or for packing on other exposed cards in downward sequence of alternate colour.

The pack is turned over one card at time. Cards that cannot be used for building or packing are put in the waste pile where they remain available until covered by the next unusable card.

A vacancy created in the top row can only be filled by an exposed king or a sequence with a king as the base card: no other sequence can be moved. If no king or king-based sequence is available, a vacancy in the top row is filled immediately by the top card in the waste pile or the next card from the stock. Vacancies in other rows can be filled by any available card whenever the player decides it is judicious to do so. Two redeals are allowed.

AS YOU LIKE IT

Deal eight packets of thirteen cards each from the shuffled packs, face downwards. Turn over the top card of each packet and lay it face up above the packet from which it came. These eight cards are called the index cards. Now turn the eight packets below the index cards face up.

Foundation cards are those one up in value from the index cards, regardless of suit and are played to a row above the index row as they become available. Foundations ascend regardless of suit. When foundations reach king, an ace is the next card to be played. Foundations are complete when the sequence reaches one below the value of the index card beneath. Thus, if there was a seven in the index row, the base card of the foundation above would be an eight which would ascend in sequence to six.

The top card of each packet in the bottom row is available. When all possible moves have been made, the left-hand packet is taken into hand, turned face downwards, and redealt from left to right, face up, onto the eight depots, starting with the now vacant left-hand one.

Continue building onto foundation piles. When no more cards can be promoted to their foundation piles, take the pile second from the left into hand, face down, and deal from left to right, face up, filling vacant spaces.

Continue in this way until each packet has been dealt out once, playing any possible cards between each deal. If the packet due to be dealt out next is exhausted, take the next one into hand for the deal.

The game comes out about once every five attempts.

BACKBONE

Shuffle each pack separately and lay one of them to the side. Deal 'the backbone' from the pack in hand, face up – two columns of ten cards each, with one card placed horizontally at its base. 'The ribs' – two columns of four cards each one on either side of the backbone – sit horizontally.

Any aces that are turned over in dealing the backbone or ribs should be played to the foundation row (where they are built on in ascending suit sequence) and the next card in turn played to the vacant space. If the twenty-first card in the deal (the base card of the backbone) is a king it is put at the bottom of the pack and the next card in turn played in its place.

After the tableau has been laid out, turn the cards from the stock over one by one. Aces and any suitable cards for building in ascending suit sequence are played as they turn up or become available in the course of play, but cards cannot be played to the foundations from the tableau unless they become available as described below. The ribs are packed in downward suit sequence but only the top cards on the bottom packets of the ribs and, at the start of the game, the base card in the backbone, can be played from the tableau to the foundation packets unless they are aces. Should the base of the backbone be played, the bottom cards in both its columns become available either for building on foundations or packing in the ribs. No packing takes place in the backbone and sequences may not be moved from rib to rib.

Vacancies in the ribs are filled at once with the top card from the pack or waste pile once it has been formed, but may not be filled from the backbone.

When the first pack is exhausted, play continues with the second pack. When there are no more cards to play, the talon is taken into hand for the only redeal permitted under the rules.

BIG FORTY

Shuffle the two packs together and deal out ten rows of four cards each. Aces are removed to the foundation row when they become available during the course of the game. The bottom card on each column is available for packing in descending suit sequence. Foundations ascend in suit sequence.

When a column becomes empty, the vacancy may be filled by any available card or sequence within the tableau or the top card in the stock.

When no more moves are possible, cards in the stock are turned over one at a time being used either for building or packing, or if neither of these are possible, cards are played to a waste pile.

When the stock is exhausted, take the talon into hand as the stock and begin to redeal without shuffling the cards. This may be done twice.

BIG WHEEL

Lay out the eight kings in a circle – the kings of hearts at twelve o'clock and six o'clock, the diamond kings at three o'clock and nine o'clock, the club kings between ten and elven o'clock and four and five o'clock and the two spade kings between one and two o'clock and seven and eight o'clock. Lay the kings in such a way that the bases form a large octogon. Then place a packet of four cards each outside each king. The top card of each packet is available. If it is an ace, two or three, it is moved into the octogon. Aces are placed on top of each other. They are surrounded by the threes pointing towards a king of their own suit. Each three in turn, has a two of the same suit played between it and the king.

The twos and threes are the foundation cards, ascending in suits of alternate number: ie, on twos are placed a four, six, eight, ten and queen of the same suit, and on threes a five, seven, nine and jack of the same suit. If the game works out, the last ace to be played to the centre of the octogon is surrounded by a ring of jacks, then a ring of matching queens with the king of the same suit beyond them.

Build available cards to foundations, filling any exhausted piles with the top card from the pack and when all possible cards have been played turn the cards in the stock over one by one. When the stock is in play, cards that cannot be used for building are played to a waste pile. If a pile becomes exhausted during play it may be filled with the top card from either the stock or the waste pile. If the top card of the waste pile is the same as the top card of a packet and one of them can be played, the card from the packet must be played.

Only when the pack is exhausted can exposed cards on the outer packets be packed in suits either in descending or ascending order. The top card of the waste pile is available for packing. There is no redeal.

THE BRITISH CONSTITUTION

Remove the kings, queens and aces from the packs, discarding seven of the queens and laying the remaining one – the monarch – in the middle of the table. Arrange the eight foundation aces in a circle, alternating red ace with black ace, around the monarch: these represent the government on which ascending suit sequences to jacks are built. Outside each ace lay a king of a different colour: red kings are the bishops, black kings represent the judiciary.

When these cards have been laid down, deal four rows of eight cards each, starting with the bottom row and working up. The lowest row represents the electorate; the one above is the House of Commons; the row above the Commons is the House of Lords, and the top row is the Privy Council. Collectively, the four rows are called the Constitution.

Cards can only be played on the foundation packets from the Privy Council. Piling takes place on the Privy Council in descending sequences of alternate colour. Any number of suitable cards can be played in a sequence. Vacancies are immediately filled by moving any card up from the row below. Vacancies that occur in the lowest row are filled at the start of the game by the top card in the pack: thereafter they may be filled either by that card or from the top card in the talon.

When all initial moves have been made, the pack

is turned over one card at a time, suitable cards being played to the Constitution according to the rules. All uncovered cards in the Constitution are available, their play releasing the card immediately below.

If the game works out, the monarch is surrounded by eight jacks who in turn are surrounded by the bishops and the judiciary.

CARLTON

Deal a row of eight cards, face up, from the shuffled packs. Overlap this row with a row of seven cards, again face up, leaving the righthand card in the first row uncovered. Continue dealing in similar fashion until the tableau is complete – eight columns, eight cards in the leftmost one, seven in the one next to it, then six, five, four, three, two and one.

The foundations are the eight aces, played to the foundation row when they become available either by becoming the exposed card in any of the columns or being turned over when the stock is in play. They ascend in suit sequence to king. Packing within the tableau is in descending sequence regardless of colour. It is within the rules to move a whole or a part-sequence onto an appropriate exposed card in the tableau. Vacancies must be filled with an exposed card from the tableau, a sequence or a part-sequence.

When all initial building and packing has been done, deal one card, face-up, onto each exposed card in the tableau and continue as before. No redeal is allowed.

CASKET

There usually comes a time in playing casket when victory seems to be well within the player's grasp – only, nine times out of ten, to have it snatched away.

Deal out a row of four cards, face up, from the shuffled packs with a reasonable space between each one. Next deal two cards above each of the left-hand and right-hand cards in the row to form the sides of the casket. Then deal the lid by dealing four cards horizontally along the top with a thirteenth card sitting vertically between the second and third cards in the lid to make the clasp. Having laid out the casket, count out thirteen cards and lay them face down in the casket to represent the jewels. (See illustration opposite.)

If there are any aces in the casket take them out and place them in the foundation zone beneath the casket. Foundations ascend in suit sequence to king. Cards in the sides and bottom of the casket may be packed in descending suit sequence. Any vacancies created in the tableau are filled with cards from the stock – the remaining cards.

The cards in the stock are turned over one by one. Suitable cards are played to the foundation packets or packed, in descending suit sequence, to the base or sides of the casket. Unusable cards are played to one of three waste piles, the top card of each being available either for building or packing.

The cards representing the lid and the clasp of the casket are not to be packed: they afford the only means of working off the jewels within the casket for whenever in the process of packing or building a suitable card is found in the lid or clasp, its vacant place is filled by one of the jewels. When the casket is empty (ie all the jewel cards have been played) vacancies created in the lid can be filled by the next card from the stock or the available cards in the waste piles.

Success in Casket depends on opening the lid as often as possible to get to the jewels, and on judicious play to the waste piles. There is no redeal.

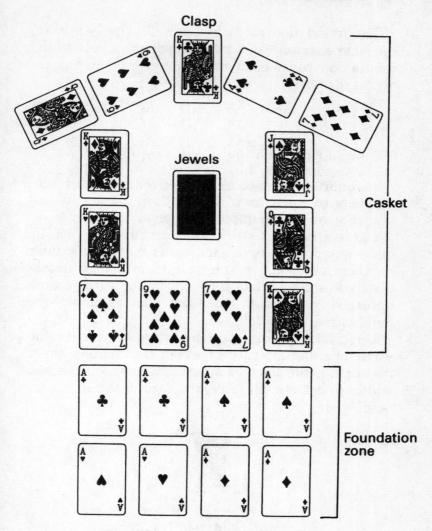

Clasp

Jewels

Casket

Foundation zone

COCK O' THE NORTH

Deal out eight packets of four cards each – four packets face up and four face down. Lay them in a star formation, alternating face up face down round its eight points (see diagram overleaf). Take the next eight cards from the stock and lay them face up in one packet in the centre of the star.

The foundation cards in Cock O' The North are the eight aces and eight twos which are played to the foundation rows as they become available and are arranged thus:

AH	AS	AD	AC
2H	2S	2D	2C
AH	AS	AD	AC
2H	2S	2D	2C

Ace foundations ascend in suit sequences of odd numbers to king: 'two' foundations ascend in suit sequence of even numbers to queen.

Cards from the stock are turned over one by one – any aces or twos (and cards that can be built on them according to the rules) are played immediately to the foundation zone. The top cards on the upturned packets in the star are available for building.

Unplayable cards from the stock are put in the waste pile, the top card of which is available. But if that card is the same as an available card in the star and both become playable, the card in the star must be played.

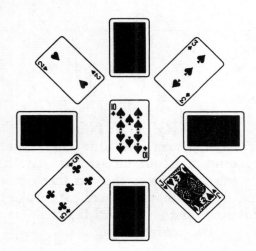

When the stock is exhausted, cards that remain in the central packet within the star are laid out – any suitable ones being played to their foundation packets. Next, the top cards of the face-down packets in the star are turned over and become available. Playing one of these does not release the card beneath! When play is blocked, all remaining cards are shuffled in with the cards in the waste pile, a new tableau is dealt and the game continues as before. Only one such redeal is allowed.

CORONA

Shuffle the packs together and deal out the first twelve cards into a circle. Then deal a second circle of twelve cards around the first twelve. The layout is completed by a third outer circle of twelve cards, so that the finished tableau looks like a corona of twelve rays each ray containing three cards.

The foundation cards are four aces of different suit and four matching kings. Ace foundations ascend in suit sequence to king: king foundations descend in suit sequence to ace. Any foundation cards that are dealt to the corona remain there until they become available.

The cards that lie at the end of each ray are all available either for building onto appropriate foundations or for packing onto other exposed cards in suit sequence, either ascending or descending. Sequences cannot be moved *en bloc* within the tableau but a suitable sequence may be played to its foundation. Vacancies can be filled by any exposed card.

When all possible building and packing has been done with the cards in the original corona and all vacancies have been filled, the stock is turned over one card at a time. Cards that cannot be packed or built can be used to fill vacancies or played to the talon. There is no redeal.

Corona gives scope for skilful card play. Aim to release foundation cards trapped within the corona as quickly as possible and make good use of the vacancies which need not be filled immediately once the deal is underway. A watchful eye on the foundations will tell how packing in the tableau is best done at any particular moment.

DEAUVILLE

Cut the shuffled packs and deal a row of ten cards, face down. Follow this with a second row of ten cards, again face down, and overlapping the cards in the row above slightly. Then a third row, again face-down, with a final row of ten cards, face-up.

Any exposed aces can be moved to the foundation row where they are built on in suit sequence to king. The card immediately above any such ace is turned over and is now available. Packing in the tableau is in descending sequence of alternate colour. Any aces or cards that can be built on aces already in the foundation row that are exposed in the course of packing are despatched to the foundation row.

Vacancies are filled by any exposed card. Sequences may not be moved, either to fill a vacancy or onto a suitable exposed card.

The cards in the stock are turned over one at a time. Aces and other suitable cards can be played directly to the foundation row. Others can be packed or put in the waste pile, the top card of which is always available. Only one deal is allowed.

DOG

Remove the eight kings from two packs of cards and line them up in a row. Shuffle the remainder of the two packs together and deal them to two rows of six cards each counting as you do so, one, two, three. . .up to queen. If in the counting any card comes out in its proper place, i.e. an ace is the first card in the top row or a six as the last card in that row, lay that card aside, face down (the dog) and continue the count on the next number. When the two rows are complete, lay three cards face down in a separate pile (the kennel) before counting out another twelve cards on top of the first two rows: continue in this way until all the cards have been dealt, always playing cards that match the count to the dog and three cards after each deal to the kennel. The more cards that are in the dog, the better the chance of getting the game out.

When all the cards have been dealt, lay out the kennel so that all are face up and available. Now begin building on the kings, downwards in suit sequence, using the top card from each packet or cards in the kennel. When play is blocked, take the top card from the dog and slip it under the packet in the tableau which matches its value: then take the top card from that packet and slip in the same way under its proper station. Continue to do so until a card is disclosed that can be played to a foundation packet. Build more cards if possible until play is again blocked at which point take the top card from the dog and play it as before. Continue in this way until the dog is exhausted.

Now gather up the packets, starting with the last one and moving backwards through the packets to the first, top left. Then place the remaining kennel cards on top of them so that they are the first cards to be dealt in the second round in which eleven packets are dealt. Lay them in a row of six cards above a row of five cards, again counting, one, two, three. . .this time up to jack and playing cards that match the count to the dog. After each count, lay four cards aside to the kennel which, after the final count, should contain sixteen cards to be laid out in four rows of four cards each. Now continue play as in the first round.

In the third round, deal the cards into ten packets playing to the dog as before, and laying five cards aside after each deal for the kennel which is laid out in two rows of five cards each.

At the end of a successsful game (a rare occurence) all the kings will have been built up to aces.

THE DUCHESS OF LUYNES

Deal out a row of four cards, face upwards, then place two cards, face downwards, alongside and on top of each other. This pair of cards form the reserve and play no part in the game at this stage. The foundation cards are four aces of different suit which are placed above the row and which ascend in suit sequence to king, and four kings of different suit which are placed below the row and which descend in suit sequence to ace. Any aces or kings which turn up in the initial deal should be played to the foundations, leaving any vacancies unfilled.

Having dealt the first round and played any suitable cards to the foundations, deal four more cards on top of the original four, filling any spaces that exist, and add two more cards, face down, to the reserve. Play any suitable cards to the foundation.

When the stock is exhausted through dealing in this way, take the reserve into hand and play any suitable cards onto the foundations, continuing to use any available cards from the tableau that become usable in playing the discard. Playing cards from the tableau releases the ones beneath.

When no more moves are possible, take the packets in the tableau into hand without shuffling them. Put the cards in the original reserve under them and redeal as before. There are three redeals and in the last one (the fourth deal) no cards are dealt to the reserve.

DUTCH

Shuffle the packs together and lay out a row of eight cards. Pack any cards if possible, in ascending order regardless of suit. Suitable sequences can be packed on top of each other. Fill any vacancies from the pack. When no more packing is possible, turn the rest of the pack over one at a time, packing if possible or playing to the waste pile. Again, fill any vacancies with either the next card in the stock or the top card in the waste pile. The eight packets in the row are said to be complete when the card next in value before the base card is reached. For example, if the base card is a three, any four can be packed on it, followed by a five and so on until the packet is topped by a two. At this point the packet is turned face down and takes no further part in the game.

Vacancies can be filled by the exposed card in another packet (or a sequence, or part-sequence), or by the top card in the stock or waste pile. There is one redeal, after which the top card only can be turned, which occasionally allows the game to work out.

EMPEROR

Deal a row of ten packets of three cards each, face down, at the top of the table. These are the sealed packets. Beneath them deal a single row of ten cards, face up. Any aces in this row are removed to the foundation row at the bottom of the table. Vacancies created in the row at this stage are filled by the next card from the pack.

When any aces (which ascend in suit sequence to

king) have been removed and the ten card row is complete, begin to pack in downward sequence of alternate colour. From now on, a vacancy created in the row is filled by the top card in the sealed packet immediately above. If that packet is exhausted, any exposed card can be moved up to fill the vacancy.

The stock is turned over one card at a time, building or packing if possible (or desirable) or discarding to the waste pile. There is no redeal, but it is permissable to move both full and part sequences onto a suitable exposed card.

The privilege of laying back is legal in Emperor. This allows a card played to a foundation to be returned to the tableau as long as it is in the right sequence. This privilege often allows a seemingly blocked game to be played out to a successful conclusion.

FORTY-NINE

Cut the shuffled packs and deal seven rows of seven cards each, the cards in each column overlapping slightly. Foundation aces dealt to the tableau remain there until they become available when all the cards covering them in the column have been played. Aces dealt to the bottom row remain their until that row is complete: only then can they be put into the foundation row. Building on the foundations is upwards in suit sequence to king. Exposed cards in the tableau can be packed either in ascending suit sequence, or in descending sequence regardless of suit. Once a sequence has been started, its direction cannot be changed. Single cards only may be moved, not sequences or part-sequences. When play in the original tableau is finished (vacant volumns can be filled by any available card but not complete sequences), the stock is turned over card by card, cards not required for building or packing being put in the waste pile, the top card of which is available.

Players are allowed the privilege of borrowing a whole foundation pile and laying it crossways on top of an exposed card in the tableau as long as the top card of the foundation is one down in value from the card on which the packet is to be laid in the tableau, regardless of suit. Any card of lower value than the top card of the moved foundation pile can be packed vertically onto it. (For example, if the top card of the borrowed foundation pile was a ten, any card from nine down to two could be packed on it.) That card can now be used as the base card for a new sequence. When all the cards packed on a borrowed foundation have been played, the foundation pile is returned *en bloc* to the foundation row. This privilege can be taken as often as possible.

When the stock is exhausted, the talon is taken into hand, face-down, and redealt without shuffling. But before it is taken into hand, players are allowed to look at the bottom card of the talon before turning it over. Thus they can see if it is better to play the exposed card in the talon (if it is playable) or to keep it there.

There is no waste pile in the second deal. All cards dealt must be played to foundations, depots or vacancies. If such a play is not possible, the game comes to an end.

FOURTEENS

The tableau for Fourteens consists of forty-eight cards laid out in the form of an open cross. This is done by dealing a row of four non-overlapping cards with a gap between the second and third cards. Below this another row of four cards is dealt, two cards on either side of the gap. Then two rows of eight cards each, four cards on either side of the gap. Now leave a horizontal gap before dealing two more rows of eight cards, four on either side of the vertical gap, finishing the tableau with two more rows of four cards each, two cards on either side of the vertical gap.

The aim of the game is to discard the entire pack. This is done by removing pairs of cards within the tableau whose total pip value is fourteen and replacing them with cards from the stock with jacks counting as eleven, queens as twelve and kings a thirteen. But paired cards must (1) lie alongside each other, (2) above and below each other, or (3) be touching at the corners. Cards can also move across the gaps according to (2) and (3) above. When pairs have been discarded, gaps are filled by moving the remaining cards in the tableau along towards the vertical gap or upwards towards the horizontal.

When pairings and movements have been completed, vacancies that remain in the tableau are filled with cards from the stock. Players should bear in mind that they do not have to discard appropriate pairs – in fact, it is often advantageous to leave them in the tableau.

FOX

Remove a king and an ace from the packs and play them to the foundation row. Thereafter foundation cards are played to the foundation row as they become available. Aces ascend in suit sequence to kings, and kings descend in suit sequence to aces.

Deal the first twenty cards from the pack, face up, in five rows of four cards each. Play suitable cards to foundations, filling vacancies created with cards from the stock. When play is blocked, deal the next twenty cards from the stock, face up, onto the twenty cards in the tableau. Continue building but leave any vacancies unfilled – cards previously dealt become available when exposed. When play comes to a halt again, deal the next twenty cards and so on until the stock is exhausted. The final deal to the tableau will probably be less than twenty cards.

Officially, there should be no redeal, but some players allow themselves the luxury of taking the cards from the tableau into hand when play is finally blocked, shuffling them and dealing a new tableau.

FRUSTRATION

Shuffle two packs together and deal eleven cards into a row. Remove any kings or aces that appear in this row putting them in a foundation row and any consecutive cards that follow suit. Ace foundations ascend in suit sequence to king, king foundations descend in suit sequence to ace. Fill any vacancies from the pack before dealing a second row of eleven cards under the top one. From now on until all the pack has been dealt into rows of eleven, no card may be played to its foundation unless it is the next card in the deal (if it is accidentally laid in the tableau, it must stay there), or it is the only card in a column. When all the cards have been laid out this rule slackens, all exposed cards (those at the bottom of each column) are available for either packing upwards or downwards in suit sequence in the tableau or onto foundation packets. It is allowable to build both ways in the tableau, e.g. a nine of hearts can be packed on a ten of hearts, on which either a jack of hearts or the other nine may be packed. Sequences cannot be moved on to another pile.

When all possible moves have been made, take the cards back into hand, starting by running down the cards in the leftmost column, then the one next to it and so on along the tableau. Lay them out in rows of eleven according to the rules. Two such redeals are allowed.

GIANT

Shuffle two packs together and lay out a row of eight cards. Any aces should be moved to the foundation rows. Foundations ascend in suit sequence to king. Any other suitable cards in the initial row can be promoted to their foundations. Cards remaining are packed downwards in alternate colours.

When all possible moves have been made, deal a second row of eight cards filling vacancies or adding to descending columns, overlapping previous cards. Exposed cards may be moved from one column to another, as can either full or part sequences (provided there is no blocking card below it) either to a vacancy in the top row or onto a card in another column ready to receive it.

It is within the rules to play a card from a foundation pile onto a suitable exposed card in the columns. This is helpful if another card can be played in sequence on it thus releasing a vital, previously blocked card.

Continue dealing successive rows of eight cards, making all possible marriages and packs before dealing each successive row. There is no redeal.

GLOUCESTERSHIRE

Shuffle the packs thoroughly before dealing them into eight rows. The top row contains ten cards, the next one, starting under the leftmost card in the top row, contains nine cards, the third, eight – and so on down to the eighth row which contains three cards.

The right hand card in each row is available for packing in descending sequence of alternate colour on any other cards in the tableau. Kings pile on aces. The foundation cards are four aces of different suits which are played to the foundation row when they become available, either as being the exposed card at the end of a row, or being turned over in playing the stock. Foundations ascend to king and then ace to king again, i.e. the thirteenth card in the heart foundation will be the king of hearts and the fourteenth will be the second ace. The stock cards are turned over one by one and unused cards become the talon.

When the game seems hopelessly blocked, top cards from the foundation packets can be played in accordance to the rule for packing back to the tableau. Vacancies that are created can be filled from the talon, the stock or by an exposed card.

There is no limit to the number of times the stock can be played, the talon being turned over and taken into hand to replace an exhausted stock.

GRAND CANYON

Deal the tableau – two rows of ten cards each, face up. The foundations are an ace and a king of each suit, played to the foundation row as they become available, aces ascending in suit sequence to king, kings descending in suit sequence to ace.

Cards in the stock are turned over one card at a time. Cards that can be built on a foundation pile are used as soon as they are turned over. Unusable cards can be played onto any of the twenty cards in the tableau, effectively creating twenty waste piles. Each card has to be used for building or played to the waste piles before the next card is turned over. The top cards of the waste piles can only be used for building. Vacancies created in the tableau must be filled immediately from the stock.

There is only one deal.

GRANDMAMA'S PATIENCE

Shuffle the two packs together and deal two rows of eleven cards each. The next card determines the foundations and is played above the leftmost card in the top row. The other foundations are three cards of different suit of the same rank played when they become available. Four more foundations, four cards of different suit one up in rank from the first four are also played to the table when they are available, put to a row beneath the tableau: e.g. if the upper row of foundation cards were eights, the lower row would be nines. The upper foundations descend in suit sequence, the lower foundations ascend in suit sequence.

Any cards that can be played to foundation rows from the tableau are put in position, vacancies being at once filled from the pack. When no further builds can be made the pondering begins!

Upon each of the cards in the tableau, you may place cards from the talon as they are turned over one by one. You may choose whichever pile you please, watching for every opportunity of building onto the foundations and filling every vacancy as soon as it occurs. There is also the privilege of taking four grace cards – i.e. you may place four cards on one side in addition to the covering cards in the rows.

It sometimes happens that when all the cards have been covered and the grace cards laid aside, no further moves are possible and the game comes to an end in which case all that can be done is to take all the cards back into hand, shuffle them thoroughly and start all over again. But usually, after covering and laying the four grace cards to one side, there are many more moves available.

HADEN

Deal the packs into twelve packets of eight cards each, face down. The remaining eight cards – the dummy – are dealt to a row, face up, beneath the twelve packets. Turn over the top card of each packet and search for pairs whose pip value totals eleven, or sequences of jack, queen, king. Discard such pairs or sequences, turn over the card beneath and continue in the same way.

Cards in the dummy can marry a card in the tableau if their combined total is eleven. If there are two face cards in the dummy that can be matched with a face card in the tableau, the three cards can be discarded, but if there are two such cards in the dummy and two in the tableau, only one can be taken from the dummy.

The aim of the game is to get rid of all the cards. If there is a choice of cards that can be matched to make the magic number, you can 'peek' at the cards beneath to see which is better to play.

HEADS AND TAILS

Shuffle two packs together before dealing out a row of eight cards. When the row has been laid on the table, count out eight packets of eleven cards each and put them under the head row. The eight remaining cards form the tail row underneath the eleven-card packets.

Aces and kings, one of each suit, are played to their respective foundation rows, kings above the head row to descend in suit sequence to aces, and aces in a row below the tail row to ascend to king.

The cards in the head and tail rows are the only ones in active play, i.e. only cards in these rows can be packed in suit sequences in either direction or promoted to their proper foundation packet. Vacancies in these two rows are filled by the top card in the packet immediately above or below. When one of the packets in the middle row becomes vacant and a vacancy occurs above or below it, the top card on the packet nearest to its left must be taken to fill it.

Packed sequences in the head and tail row can be unloaded – i.e. if a ten has been packed down to a five in the head row and a four turns up in the tail row, or vice versa, the five and as many cards on the sequence as is wanted can be transferred onto the four. This often proves useful in freeing cards that are needed for building on foundations.

Once a card has been played to the foundation row it cannot be moved.

HENRY THE EIGHTH

Remove the eight kings and one ace of hearts from the packs and position them in three rows of three cards each. In the top row, one heart king sits between the two spade kings. In the middle row, the second king of hearts sits between the two kings of diamonds. And in the bottom row, the ace of hearts is flanked by the kings of clubs. The foundation cards are the seven kings and the ace that surround the central king of hearts. Foundations ascend in suit sequence to queen, the seven foundation kings being first covered by suitable aces.

Deal two columns of four cards each, one on either side of the foundation tableau. These constitute the divans and cards within them can be played onto foundations if possible. Having done so proceed to turn over the cards from the stock one by one, playing suitable cards to their foundations, discarding cards that cannot be played to the waste heap, the top card of which is available.

Vacancies in the divans are filled by cards from the stock or from the talon, but such spaces need not be filled as soon as they occur.

If the game works out, and two redeals are allowed, the central king of hearts – Henry VIII – is surrounded by eight queens; his six wives and his two daughters who became queen in turn.

HUSSAR

Deal twenty-four cards in three rows of eight cards each. Any aces that turn up in laying out the tableau (or in subsequent play) are discarded as they play no part in the game. By moving the cards according to the rules of the game, the aim is to have the top row consisting entirely of twos, the middle row with all the threes and the bottom row with the fours. These become the foundation cards on which ascending suit sequences in intervals of three are built, so that if the game works out, the top cards in the packets in the top row are all jacks, the centre row is topped by queens and the bottom row by kings. Building on each foundation packet can begin as soon as a foundation two, three or four is in its proper row.

Suppose in the original tableau there is an ace in the centre row and another in the bottom row. Both these cards are discarded, any four in the layout moved to the vacant space in the bottom row and any three to the space in the centre row.

When all available moves have been made, deal the top eight cards from the stock to a waste pile at the foot of each column, discarding any ace that turns up. Cards in these waste piles can be played to suitable foundations or used to fill spaces in the layout. The game continues until the stock is exhausted, the top card of each waste pile always being available.

INTRIGUE

Shuffle the two packs together and remove any queen. Put her to the left of the table. Pile cards from the pack on top of her until the next queen turns up. Lay her alongside the first queen-based pile and pile the next cards from the pack onto the second queen until the third queen turns up and so on until there is a row of eight queen-based piles on the table. All fives and sixes that turn up in the deal are put in two foundation rows, sixes below the tableau and fives above it.

Build up to jacks, regardless of suit, on the sixes, and down to kings (which are built on top of aces) on the fives.

The top cards of the queen-based piles are all available for building and for packing on each other either in descending or ascending order, regardless of suit. When a queen comes into view, all the cards on her pile having been played to foundations or packed on another pile, any exposed card can be used to cover her, or she can remain uncovered. If the game comes out, an event that happens about once every three games, the table will show a row of queens sandwiched between a row of jacks and a row of kings.

THE ISLE OF CAPRI

Take an ace and a king of each suit from the packs and lay them in the centre of the table as the foundations. Aces ascend in suit sequence to king: kings descend in suit sequence to aces.

Deal a row of six cards, four face up (the tableau) and two face down (the reserve). Build on the foundations if possible before dealing a second row of six cards, four face up, covering the cards that remain in the tableau or filling any vacancies that have been created, with two face down to the reserve. Continue building and dealing in this way until all the cards in the stock have been played.

At this point take the 32 cards in the reserve into hand and turn them over one by one. Suitable cards from the reserve are played to the foundation. This should create more opportunites for building from the tableau.

When no further play is possible, take the cards

from the tableau into hand along with unplayed cards from the reserve, shuffle them thoroughly and redeal as before. The number of cards in the reserve at the end of the second deal will depend on how well play has progressed during the first round.

A third deal is allowed in which no cards are dealt to reserves.

KINGS

Remove the eight aces and play them to two foundation columns, aces of spades at the top above the aces of hearts, then the aces of diamonds with the aces of clubs at the bottom. The foundations are build upwards to kings irrespective of suit. Shuffle the rest of the pack and deal four rows of two cards each to the left of the foundation zone and four rows of two cards each to the right of it; the left and right depots respectively. Available cards are those at the outside of the rows. During the deal, they can be used for building only if they are in a depot alongside its appropriate foundation. So, an exposed card from the right depot can only be played to the right-hand foundation column in the same row, and similarly with exposed cards in the left hand depots.

When all possible building has been done with the tableau cards, deal one more card to each row, starting with the top left, working down the rows, then up to the top right and down. Play any available cards that are turned up during this deal according to the rule, replacing them with the next card to be dealt. Continue in the same way until the stock is exhausted. Now the rules for building change.

Available cards can be built on any foundation pile as long as they are in ascending sequence regardless of suit. Exposed cards can also be packed on each other, either in downward or upward sequence, irrespective of suit, thus releasing cards trapped in the depots. Sequences cannot be moved. Vacant rows may be filled by any exposed card.

There is no redeal.

LE ROUGE ET LE NOIR

Take the aces from the packs and lay them in a row in the foundation zone. They are built upwards in suit sequence to kings.

Deal a row of eight cards, face up. Cards in this row can be built on foundation packets if possible, or packed on each other in descending sequence of alternate colour. Only one card at a time may be packed: packed sequences may not be moved. Vacancies in the row must be filled immediately from the stock or the top card from the waste pile once it is created.

The stock is turned over one card at a time: cards that cannot be used for building or packing are put into the waste pile. When the stock is exhausted, the waste pile is turned over unshuffled for one redeal.

LUCAS

Remove the eight aces and lay them in the foundation row. Beneath them deal thirteen columns of three cards each. The bottom cards are available either for building on the foundations or for packing within the tableau – both are in suit sequence, ascending in the foundations, descending in the tableau. Vacant columns can be filled by any available card or sequence.

When all possible moves have been made on the tableau or foundations, cards from the stock are turned over one by one. Suitable cards can be built on foundations or packed in the tableau. Unused are put in the waste pile, the top card of which is available for building or packing. There are two redeals.

MISS MILLIGAN

This is one of the classic two-pack patiences. Deal a row of eight cards, removing any aces that are dealt to the foundation row and filling the space created with the next card from the pack. Foundations ascend in suit sequence to king. Pack any exposed cards in the eight-card row in descending sequences of alternate colour.

When all builds and packs have been made, deal a second eight card row, each card within it overlapping the one above it slightly, or filling any vacancies in the top row created during play.

The second row must be completed before any more builds and packs can be made. The game continues in this way, building and packing after each new row of eight cards has been dealt. Vacant columns can only be filled by a king or a sequence with a king as the base card. Sequences can only be moved intact.

After the whole stock has been dealt, a card at the bottom of a column that blocks a sequence can be taken into hand as a reserve and held there until it can be played to the tableau. Only one card at a time may be removed — a concession known as waiving.

NAPOLEON'S FAVOURITE

Whether or not the Little Emperor whiled away his years in exile on St Helena playing this game is not recorded, but it is an interesting and not-too-challenging game nonetheless.

The two packs are not shuffled together but are played one after the other. An ace and a king of each suit are removed from the first pack and laid in two foundation rows, kings above matching aces. Then beginning above the left hand king, twelve cards are dealt in a clockwise direction, one above each king, one at the right hand end of both rows, one below each ace and one at the left hand end of each row.

Foundations ascend in suit sequence to king on the ace foundations and descend in suit sequence to ace on the kings. In the early stages of the game only cards in the row above the kings can be played on king foundation piles. Similarly only cards in the row beneath the aces can be played on ace foundation piles. Cards lying at the end of each row may be played on either.

Tableau cards can also be built on each other, regardless of suit in either direction. The sequence may be reversed in the same pile, but only a queen may be built on a king and only a two on an ace.

Once all possible builds have been made, spaces are filled from the stock, again in a clockwise direction starting with the leftmost space in the top row. Play continues until there are twelve unbuildable cards surrounding the foundation rows at which point twelve cards are dealt from the stock, one on top of each waste pile.

When both packs have been exhausted the rules change. Suitable top cards from any waste pile can be played on either foundation row and the top card in each waste pile can be packed in either descending or ascending order regardless of suit, thus releasing cards within the waste piles.

When play is blocked, the waste piles are taken into hand anticlockwise starting with the pile at the left end of the top row and placed face downwards so that the bottom card of the first pile taken into hand becomes the top card in the new stock. A total of three deals is allowed.

NAPOLEON'S SHOULDER

Deal twelve packets of four cards each and position them on the table face up to form three sides of a square – two columns placed vertically on the table and one horizontal row along the top. Make sure the square is large enough to house the eight aces – the foundations which ascend in suit sequence to king.

Play any suitable available cards from the square to the foundation packets before beginning to pack the piles in the square in descending sequence regardless of suit. As usual, only the top card of each packet is available, its removal releasing the card immediately below. But unusually, it is within the rules to examine all the cards in the packets. If, in doing this, one packet is found to contain two kings of the same suit on top of two lower cards of that suit, the whole tableau can be redealt or one of the kings may be put to the bottom of the packet.

The stock is turned over one card at a time, unsuitable cards being played to the talon, the top card of which is available. When a vacancy occurs in the square it is filled either by the top card of the stock or the top card of the talon, but such vacancies need not be filled immediately.

There is only one deal.

Another version of Napoleon's Shoulder is played in exactly the same way, but only one card is dealt to each packet in the square at the beginning.

NEW YORK! NEW YORK!

Shuffle the two packs together before laying out a row of eight cards. The ninth card is the first foundation and is placed above the row. The other seven foundations are the cards of similar rank and are played to the foundation row when they become available in the course of play.

Foundations ascend in suit sequence, the final card in each foundation being the one immediately below the base foundation card in rank. Columns in the tableau are packed downwards in alternate colours.

Now turn over the pack one card at a time, playing to foundations or packing in the tableau if possible. Useless cards are played to any of three talons. Vacant columns that are created in the course of play need not be filled immediately and when it is decided to fill them, the exposed card in any of the three talons may be used to do so.

There is only one deal: success in the game depends on how the waste piles are manipulated: it is best to keep one waste pile exclusively for court cards, which would block lower cards needed to build onto foundations during the early stages.

NORTH AND SOUTH

Lay the four black kings in a cross – the two kings of clubs as the upright, the two kings of spades as the arms. Complete the cross with an ace of hearts above and below the kings of clubs, one ace of diamonds to the left of the left-hand king of spades. Next, an ace of spades is laid crossways above the top ace of hearts and an ace of clubs crossways below the lower heart ace. And finally, a king of hearts and a king of diamonds, vertically at either end of either arm of the cross – the heart king to the left and the diamond king to the right.

These last four cards are the barrier cards. Starting just above the king of hearts, deal three cards between each barrier. The three cards between the heart king and the spade ace represent the Europeans. The three between the spade ace and the diamong king represent the Asians. Collectively the two races make up the Northern Hemisphere. The cards between the diamond king and club ace represent the Australians and those between the club ace and heart king are the Africans. The Australians and the Africans represent the Southern Hemisphere.

The four black kings and red aces are the foundation cards, aces ascending in suit sequence to king, kings descending in suit sequence to ace.

Red cards represent the races of the Northern Hemisphere: black cards represent those of the Southern Hemisphere.

Once the foundations, barriers and first twelve cards representing the four races have been dealt, build, pack and exchange available cards in accordance with the following rules.

1 Only cards that belong to their proper hemispheres are available.

2 Cards of the wrong colours may be exchanged into their proper hemispheres whenever the opportunity occurs and at the end of the game when all the cards are dealt and the talon is exhausted, they may be transferred without an exchange.

3 Cards may only 'marry' those belonging to their own 'race', but cards from the talon may 'marry' any 'race'.

4 The barriers cannot be moved till the end of the game, when they are played to complete the foundations.

5 All the foundations must follow suit.

Having made all available builds, packs and exchanges, fill any vacancies that have been created in the tableau, proceeding clockwise from the card above the king of hearts, and then turn cards from the pack over one by one, building, packing and exchanging whenever the opportunity occurs or playing to the talon, the top card of which is always available. Fill any vacancies with the top card from the pack or talon as they are created. Sequences and part-sequences may be moved in accordance with the rules. There is no redeal.

OLD CALEDONIA

Shuffle the two packs together and lay out the top eight cards into two columns of four cards each, leaving enough space between the columns to house the foundation cards, an ace and king of each suit lying horizontally alongside each other. They are played to the foundation zone when they turn up in the course of play. Aces ascend in suit sequence to king, king foundations descend in suit sequence to ace. If suitable kings or aces appear in dealing the two columns (and other cards that can be properly played to the foundations), put them in the foundation zone right away, dealing the next card in turn to fill the vacancy.

When the columns are complete, arrange four groups of three fanned cards each in a column to the outside of the two original columns, four fans in each column. The top card of each fan is available for building or packing in downward sequence of alternate colour either on to an exposed card in another fan or on to a suitable card in the column alongside. Packing in both cases is downwards in alternate colours. The cards in the two columns can only be played to foundations. A card played from a fan on to a card in the rows may not be played to the fans at a later stage.

When a vacancy occurs in either of the columns it is filled by one of the exposed cards in the fans that lie alongside that column, but it need not be filled immediately. If a fan becomes empty in the course of building and packing, the top three cards are taken from the pack to replace them.

There is one privilege: to place an available card from the fans, according to suit and in either upward or downward sequence, upon any of the cards in the columns. But a card so played cannot be moved until it is played to its foundation packet.

When all possible builds and packs have been made, cards that remain in the fans are gathered up and put to one side. New fans are dealt from the pack and play proceeds as before. Thereafter, all the cards in the stock and discarded fans are shuffled together before each subsequent redeal. Players are allowed as many redeals as they wish before they recognize defeat or the game comes out.

ORDER

Take any six from the pack and lay it in the centre of the table as the first foundation. The other foundations are the first seven, eight, nine, ten, jack, queen and king that become available in the course of play according to the rule that no foundation card can be played unless the one immediately below it in rank is in position: i.e. if the six, seven, eight and nine are in the foundation and the jack turns up, it cannot be played as a ten has not yet been played to the foundation zone.

The foundations ascend in sequence regardless of suit or colour, aces being built on king and the sequence continuing with the two.

The stock is turned over one card at a time. Unplayable cards are put in the waste pile, the top card of which is available. Two redeals are allowed with the cards in the waste pile being thoroughly shuffled between deals.

PAGANINI

Deal all the cards into eight rows of thirteen cards each, leaving a space between each card. If the game works out, each of the rows form a complete suit, ace at the left rising to king at the right. The game begins by moving any ace to the left-hand end of a row thus creating a space in the tableau which must be filled by the next highest card of the same suit as the card on the left of the space. This in turn creates another space which is filled in the same way. Runs are brought to an end when a space is created on the right hand side of a king there being no appropriate card to fill the space. At this point another ace is moved to the left-hand end of a row.

The skill in playing Paganini lies in deciding which ace to play to the beginning of which row and, as there are two of each card in the layout, which of the appropriate pair to move to fill vacant spaces. By the time all eight aces have been moved to the start of the rows (and assuming that no suit sequence is complete) there will be eight vacancies to fill in the tableau with a choice of two cards to fill each of them.

PRINCESS PATIENCE

Whichever princess devised this game, she must have had a great deal of time on her hands because the cards have to be laid over and over again if the player is to have any chance of getting out.

Shuffle the two packs together and deal four rows of four cards each to the left of the table, starting on the outside and working inwards. On the right side of the table, deal in similar fashion four more rows of four cards each, dealing towards the centre of the table. Make sure that there is enough space betwen the two blocks of cards to house the eight aces – the foundation cards on which cards are built in ascending suit sequence to king.

The only cards that can be moved at the beginning of the game are those in the two innermost columns, they can be played to the foundation or packed on other cards in their own wing of the tableau in descending suit sequence.

Thereafter cards can only be moved if there is no card lying between them and the foundation zone.

Cards from the pack are turned over one by one and either played to the foundations or packed in the tableau if possible according to the rules. Unplayable cards are played to the waste pile.

When a vacancy occurs anywhere in the tableau it can be filled by the top card in the waste pile, or any exposed king in the tableau can be moved into it, his place being taken by the next card in the pack. Vacancies do not have to be filled immediately and it is often advantageous to leave them free. When an entire row is vacant it can be refilled either by cards from the pack or cards from the waste pile.

The game is played out in only one deal.

REFORM

Deal a row of eleven cards, face upwards, from the shuffled packs. Now remove one ace and one king from the stock and play them to the foundation row. The other foundation cards are three other aces of different suits and three other kings of different suits. Aces ascend in suit sequence to king; kings descend in suit sequence to ace.

Build any suitable cards from the row onto the foundation cards. Fill vacancies, left to right, build again if possible and so on until the game is blocked.

A second row is now dealt, face up, each card overlapping the card above. From now only the leftmost card in a row or the two rightmost ones are available (apart from aces and kings which are played to foundation – but only after the row is complete). Vacancies that occur by playing cards to the foundation piles must be filled left to right before the next row is dealt. Cards dealt to vacancies in the leftmost column and the two rightmost ones may be played if possible and the vacancy refilled; those that fill vacancies in columns created by playing a foundation ace or king are not to be played.

Once the pack has been dealt in this way, the card at the bottom of each column is available for building or for packing which in Reform is either in ascending or descending suit sequence. It is within the rules to change the direction of a sequence whenever necessary, but sequences may not be moved.

Vacant rows may be (but do not have to be) filled by any exposed card. When play is blocked take all the cards in the tableau into hand, running down the leftmost column and continuing along the tableau so that when the cards are turned over the cards in the leftmost column are at the bottom of the pack when it is redealt. One redeal is allowed.

ROUND ROBIN

Deal a row of four cards, beneath it a row of five, followed by rows of six, seven, eight, seven, six, five and four cards to create a barrel shaped tableau of fifty-two cards. There must be a one-card space between each card, so that the cards in one row touch the cards in the rows above and below at the corners.

The object is to move the cards in the tableau so that an ace and a king of each suit occupy the centre row of eight cards – now the foundation row. Foundations ascend in suit sequence on the aces and descend, also in suit sequence, on the kings.

Packing within the tableau is in either descending or ascending order in alternate colour, but only cards that have two or more corners free can be moved, so at the beginning of the game the only cards that can be moved are those in the top and bottom rows and the cards at either end of the centre, eight-card row. Cards with only one corner free may be packed on. Packed sequences may not be moved in part and can only be repacked onto a single card.

If the top cards of two same-suit foundations are in sequence any or all of the cards in either foundation pile may be moved onto the other, leaving the base card in its original position.

The 52-card stock is turned over one card at a time: if they cannot be played to a foundation packet or used for packing, they are played to the waste pile the top card of which is, as usual, available.

Vacancies in the layout are filled from the stock after further play is impossible and before the next card from the stock is turned over for play. Such spaces must be filled from left to right starting in the top row and working downwards. One redeal is allowed.

ROYAL COTILLION

A cotillion was a formal pattern dance much enjoyed in the eighteenth century at the French king's court. The formal layout of the tableau in Royal Cotillion is similar to one of the patterns of the dance, hence the name of the game.

Remove one ace and one two of each suit from the pack and shuffle the cards. Lay the aces in a column – the ace of spades at the top, with the ace of hearts below it, the ace of diamonds below it and with the ace of clubs at the bottom. Place the matching twos in a similar column to the right of the aces, with a card space between the two columns.

When the foundation cards are in position, deal twelve cards in three rows of four cards each to the left of the aces so that the three top aces sit at the right-hand end of each row with the ace of clubs lying alone. This is the left wing. Now deal the right wing – four rows of four cards each to the right of the twos so that each two sits at the left-hand end of a row.

The foundation piles are built up in twos: three, five, seven. . . to king on the aces, four, six, eight. . . to queens on the twos. In the left wing, only the bottom card of each column can be played to a foundation pile and the spaces so created remain vacant; in the right wing any card can be built on a suitable foundation and the spaces created are filled with either the top card of the waste pile or the next card in the stock which is turned over card by card. Cards from the stock that cannot be played to a foundation pile or used to fill a space in the right wing are put, face up, in the waste heap. There is no sequence building on either wing.

There is no redeal.

SALIC LAW

Salic law is one whereby women have no rights of succession so it is to be expected that queens play no part in this game! As they appear in the course of play they are placed in a row above the eight foundation aces which ascend in sequence regardless of suit to jacks. If the game comes out, the row of eight queens sits above a row of eight packets the top card of each being a jack, with all the kings in a row along the bottom.

Start by removing one king from the pack and laying it on the left of the table. On this king place all cards as they are dealt until the second king appears. It is placed alongside the first packet and cards are dealt on it until the third king appears, and so on until the last king is dealt and all remaining cards are heaped on it. Any aces that are dealt are immediately put in the foundation row and any subsequent suitable cards piled on as they turn up. Any queens are placed above them.

All the cards on the surface of the eight king packets are available to be played to appropriate foundations, the playing of the top card releasing the card beneath it.

Play any surface cards to appropriate foundation packets, in doing so hoping to free some of the kings entirely, for when all cards on top of a king have been played, one card (the top card of any of the other packets) can be played onto it. It is, of course, best to play a card on a vacant king that releases the greatest number of suitable cards to foundations and to this end it is permissible at any time to examine the contents of the king-based packets.

No redeal is allowed.

S-S-S-SNAKE (1)

Take out a full sequence regardless of suit and lay them in an ascending s-shape with the seven at the tail and the six at the other end. Deal the cards from the pack one at a time, packing suitable cards in ascending order onto the tableau, regardless of suit, and discarding unplayable cards into either of two waste piles, the top two cards of both of these being available. No redeal is allowed. The seven at the base of the S is built up to ace, the eight next to it is built up to two, the nine above that is built up to three and so on, so that if the game comes out, the snake has an ace at its tail to a king at its head.

S-S-S-SNAKE (2)

The difference between this game and S-S-S-Snake (1) is that the snake is built up in suits according to rotation – diamond, spades, hearts and clubs. Lay out the figure in diamonds, play as for Snake (1) remembering that diamonds are covered by spades which in turn are covered by hearts, then clubs then diamonds again. . .

Cards from the pack that cannot be played may be played into any of four waste piles. If the game comes out (and although players are allowed two redeals it seldom does) the final snake will show a complete ascending sequence of clubs.

SQUADRON LEADER

Deal four rows of ten cards each, face up, the cards in each column overlapping slightly. Lay three cards horizontally in a column, also face up, to the right of the right-hand column of the tableau. This column is the reserve.

The available cards at this stage are the bottom cards of each column, the three cards in the reserve, and the top card of the stock which is turned over.

The foundations are the eight aces which are moved to the foundation row when they become available. They ascend in suit sequence to king. The stock is turned over card by card, unplayable cards being put in the waste pile, the top card of which is always available.

Vacant columns need not be filled immediately, but when there is a vacancy in the reserve it must be filled immediately by any available card.

Exposed cards in the tableau can be packed on each other in descending order of alternate colour. Sequences and part-sequences can also be moved. Cards in the stock can only be used for building.

There is no redeal.

STAG PARTY

Shuffle the packs together and deal the cards into rows of eight cards each. When fives and sixes are turned up, remove them to the foundation columns, the fives to the right of the tableau, the sixes to the left. Foundations are built in suits, the fives down to kings, via aces and the sixes up to jacks.

After each row is dealt, examine the tableau to see if any available cards can be played to appropriate foundations. Available cards are those at the bottom of each column and those above a gap in the tableau – vacancies are not filled.

Queens, being unwelcome at any stag party are discarded – the vacancies created remaining empty in accordance with the rules.

STREETS AHEAD

Deal four rows of ten cards, face up, from the shuffled packs. The foundation cards are the eight aces which are moved to the foundation row when they become available after the tableau has been completed.

Move any aces in the bottom row to the foundation zone and build any available cards – the exposed cards at the bottom of each column – on them. Foundations ascend in suit sequence to king.

Packing in the tableau is downwards in alternate colour. Only single cards, not sequences, may be moved.

When all possible building and packing has been done (vacant columns being filled by any exposed card at the player's discretion) the cards from the stock are turned over one by one. Cards that cannot be used for building or packing are played to the waste pile, the top card of which is available.

There is no redeal.

THOR'S HAMMER

According to Norse mythology, Thor was Woden's eldest son and God of Thunder. Whenever he threw his hammer it came back to him, boomerang fashion. His hammer gives its name to this game, though why is lost in the mists of time, for although the foundation aces are collectively referred to as

Thor's Hammer, they are laid in the shape of a swastika.

Remove all the aces from the packs before shuffling the cards. The aces are laid out as follows: the two aces of hearts sit vertically, one on top of the other with a card's width between them: the two aces of clubs sit horizontally, touching the heart aces at the corners: the aces of spades are laid horizontally, one above and one below both heart aces, forming a reverse swastika; the two aces of diamonds are placed vertically alongside the club aces to complete the swastika (*see diagram*).

The top nine cards from the stock are now laid out, face up, in a triangular shape, three cards forming each side of the triangle. Aces are built on in ascending suit sequence to nines: cards in the triangle can be packed on each other downwards regardless of suit (although if there is a choice, pack in suits as it can help the game to come out).

Vacancies in the triangle caused either by packing or by playing a suitable card to foundation, are filled in the first instance by cards from the stock. Thereafter, when the stock is in play, either by cards from the stock, or by the exposed cards in other packets in the triangle.

When no more cards from the first triangle can be played, deal nine more cards from the stock onto the triangle. It seldom happens that each ace is built to nine by the time the stock has been completely played, but there is still a chance to get out. Gather all the unplaced cards in the triangle and talon (the top card of which has always been available) and take them into hand. The stock is now played to a different shaped tableau – this time made up of two columns of three cards each. Building and packing are as before. At the end of each play, deal another six cards to the columns. This is the last chance, for if after this second round has been completed, all the foundations have not been built up to ace, the cards win!

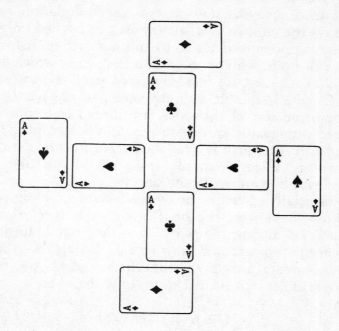

TOAD

Deal thirteen cards from the stock, face up, into a reserve pile. Remove any aces that are dealt to the reserve and put them in the foundation row, topping up the reserve as necessary. If no ace turns up, remove one from the stock and put it in the foundation row. The remaining seven aces are played to the foundation row as they become available. They are built upwards to king, regardless of suit or colour.

The stock is turned over one card at a time. Unplayable cards are put into any of five talons. The top card of the reserve and those of the waste piles are always available. There is no redeal.

UNCLE WALTER

Shuffle the two packs and deal out three rows of twelve cards. Proceed to pack in downward suit sequence, playing any aces to the foundation row above the tableau. But, a card may be packed only if it has to be moved across to another card on its own row or up to a higher row than the one in which it is laid. Vacancies are filled by cards from the stock.

Once all suitable building and packing has been done, the rest of the cards are turned over one by one. Unplayable cards are put in a waste pile, the top card of which is available. Vacancies in the top row are filled by cards from the waste pile or tableau, but not from the pack.

Officially there is no redeal, but some players allow themselves the privilege of 'the turn of the card' i.e. taking the waste pile into hand, turning over the top card and playing it if possible. But there is no waste pile in this unofficial redeal: the first unplayable card turned over stops the game.

UP AND DOWN

Shuffle each pack independently and lay one of them to the side for the time being. Turn over the top card of the pack in hand and lay it on the table. The foundation cards are the four cards of different suit immediately above it in value and the four immediately below it in value. The higher foundations ascend in suit sequence, the lower ones descend in suit sequence. The card that determines the foundations stays where it is on the table and is covered by others of the same value when they are turned over in the course of play.

Cards from the stock are turned over one by one: cards that cannot be built onto the foundations are played to any of four waste piles: the top card of each waste pile is always available.

When the first pack is exhausted, take the second pack into hand and continue to turn the cards over in the same way. Cards of the same value as the original turn up card are played to that pile: cards of the same value as the foundation cards are played to the waste pile, unless they can be used for building.

Whenever, in the course of building, one of the packets reaches the turn-up card, the card necessary to complete the suit sequence is taken from that pile and played on the now-finished packet.

When the second pack is exhausted, the waste piles are gathered up and played through once more without being shuffled.

One privilege is allowed. Cards can be moved from one of the ascending foundation packets to one of the descending ones (and vice versa) if the cards at the top of the two piles are consecutive. This is useful as it can help release vital, blocked cards in the waste pile.

VACUUM

Nine times out of ten, this patience fails: on the few times that it does come out, the sense of achievement at extricating the cards from their entanglements is very satisfying.

The two packs are not shuffled together. Remove the aces and kings from one pack and place them in a row with the aces to the left and the kings to the right of a space large enough to house a row of three cards. This is the vacuum. The aces and kings are the foundations, aces ascending to kings and kings descending to aces, both in suit sequence. Next deal the top eleven cards from the first pack into a row, one card under each of the foundation cards with three cards beneath the vacuum.

Continue dealing cards into rows of eleven cards under the first one, each card overlapping slightly with the one above. When all the cards in the first pack have been laid down, continue the rows with the cards from the second pack.

If, in forming the rows, a card turns up *directly* under an ace or king on which it can be suitably played, it may be put in position at once, the next card in the pack taking its place in the tableau. Cards laid in the spaces under the vacuum can be played to either side and any uncovered card that follows may also be taken. For example, if a two is uncovered it may be put on its ace, and a three, if uncovered, may follow it, provided they are under the vacuum.

As soon as all the cards are dealt out this restriction ceases and uncovered cards can be played to suitable foundations and may also be packed on one another in upward and downward sequence following suit.

A vacant lane can be filled by any uncovered card or sequence of cards. Suitable exposed cards may be moved from one column to another (but sequences may not), and the same can be done with the top cards in the ace and king packets if it helps to further the game.

When the game is blocked, run the first column together without shuffling, lay it on the second, which is also run together and so on until all the cards in the columns have been taken into hand. Lay them out again in columns of eleven, observing the same rules as before. This may be done once more and then, if the game has still not come out. . .no wonder Nature abhors a vacuum: so, all to frequently, do patience players in this game!

THREE-AND FOUR-PACK GAMES

BARTON

Shuffle four packs together and lay out six rows of seventeen cards each. Any aces in the bottom row should be removed to the foundation zone. Foundations ascend in suit sequence to king.

The stock is turned over one card at a time. Suitable cards should be played to the foundation zone or packed on available cards in the tableau in descending suit sequence. But it is not wise to pack too freely at the beginning of the game as vital cards can become blocked in a sequence.

Available cards in the tableau (those at the bottom of a column) can only be packed on a suitable card if the suitable card is in a higher row; e.g. if a column contains two cards, the exposed one being the eight of diamonds, and the nine of diamonds was the exposed card of a four-card row, the eight can not be packed on the nine: but if the nine of diamonds was the exposed card in a two-card row and the eight of diamonds was the exposed card in a four card row, the eight could then be packed on to the nine. When a vacancy occurs in the top row, it can be filled by any exposed card.

Cards from the stock that cannot be played are put in the waste pile, the top card of which is always available.

There is no redeal and although the game seldom comes out, it is deservedly popular. Experienced players consider it a victory if they succeed in building eight aces up to king!

CABLE PATIENCE

This game comes out about once every twenty attempts, but just because nineteen games have been played and lost, there is no guarantee that the next will come out.

The three packs are shuffled individually: they represent three cables, the object of the game being to twine them together. The first pack is laid out in five rows of ten cards each. The remaining two cards are put face down to one side – as the fortune-teller's surprise. Continue the rows with the second pack, again discarding the last two cards unseen to the fortune-teller.

Packing and building now begins. Exposed cards in the tableau can be packed on one another in downward suit sequence. Aces that become available are removed to the foundation row and built up to their respective kings. Exposed cards can be freely moved from one column to another, and whole sequences may be moved if there is a suitable card on which to pack them. Part sequences may also be moved.

When all preliminary packing and building has been done, the third pack is taken into hand and turned over card by card, unplayable cards being put in the waste pile, the top card of which is available.

If a vacancy is created in the top row, any exposed card can fill it, or a sequence (or part-sequence) can be moved up into it.

There is one redeal after which the surprise cards lying with the fortune-teller are turned over, one by one. The fortune-teller's hand often contains the cards necessary to unblock the game which goes on until all the foundations are complete or there is no alternative but to admit defeat, take all the cards into hand, sort them into three packs and start all over again.

GETAWAY

Shuffle three packs together and lay out a tableau of six rows of eight cards each. One set of aces (one of each suit) and two sets of kings (two of each suit) turned over are played to foundations immediately and the vacancy is filled by the next card in turn. The aces (which ascend in suit sequence) are played to a row above the tableau: the kings (which descend in suit sequence) are laid in horizontal rows, two sets on either side of the tableau. Foundation cards trapped within the packs are played to the foundation zones when they become available.

The bottom cards of each row in the tableau are available and after any suitable ones have been played to foundations (there is no packing within the tableau in Getaway) the stock is turned over one card at a time, unplayable cards being put in the waste pile. A vacancy that occurs in the top row in the tableau is filled with any exposed card in the tableau.

When the stock is exhausted, the talon is turned over for the only redeal permitted. Good judgement and constant observation of the foundation packets are essential, but even so, the game seldom comes out.

INDEX